SpringerBriefs in Computer Science

More information about this series at http://www.springer.com/series/10028

Eric Nunes • Paulo Shakarian • Gerardo I. Simari
Andrew Ruef

Artificial Intelligence Tools for Cyber Attribution

 Springer

Eric Nunes
Arizona State University
Tempe, AZ, USA

Paulo Shakarian
Arizona State University
Tempe, AZ, USA

Gerardo I. Simari
Department of Computer Science
and Engineering
Universidad Nacional del Sur (UNS) &
Institute for Computer Science and
Engineering (UNS-CONICET)
Bahia Blanca, Argentina

Andrew Ruef
University of Maryland
College Park, MD, USA

ISSN 2191-5768   ISSN 2191-5776   (electronic)
SpringerBriefs in Computer Science
ISBN 978-3-319-73787-4   ISBN 978-3-319-73788-1   (eBook)
https://doi.org/10.1007/978-3-319-73788-1

Library of Congress Control Number: 2017963778

Printed on acid-free paper

This Springer imprint is published by Springer Nature
The registered company is Springer International Publishing AG
The registered company address is: Gewerbestrasse 11, 6330 Cham, Switzerland

Acknowledgements

The authors would like to acknowledge the generous support from the U.S. Department of the Navy, Office of Naval Research Grant: N00014-15-1-2742 (in particular, Sukarno Mertoguno), Arizona State University Global Security Initiative (in particular, Nadya Bliss and Jamie Winterton), funds provided by Universidad Nacional del Sur and CONICET, Argentina, the National Science Foundation, the Army Research Office under the Science of Security Lablet grant (SoSL), and the DARPA URAP project (in particular, Dan Ragsdale). We would also like to thank the following collaborators who have contributed in some of the research discussed in the book (in no particular order): Nimish Kulkarni, Jay Little, Geoffrey Moores, Damon Paulo, Simon Parsons, Marcelo Falappa, and Ashkan Aleali.

Contents

Chapter 1
Introduction

Cyber attribution is the process by which the identity of an actor or aggressor in a cyberactivity is determined. Conducting this process presents several unique problems; chief among them are that the technical artifacts produced by cyberattacks are difficult to understand, and it is easy (and quite useful) for an actor to perform deception.

The process, flaws, outcomes, and methodology of cyber attribution have become a subject of increasingly broad interest over the past few years. Part of this is due to the increase in cyberactivity and the intersection of that cyberactivity with the public sphere. For example, it used to be that a major company being hacked would be of concern only to that company and its customers; however, the compromise of Sony Pictures allegedly by North Korea in late 2014 elevated public interest in the accurate attribution of cyberaggression to the national level.

The analysis that underpins cyber attribution involves many diverse sources of data: network forensics, host forensics, malware analysis, and code similarity, to name a few. Like intelligence analysis, independent and diverse sources of reporting strengthen an analytic argument. In cybersecurity, an adversary might find that they have complete control over which hosts they use across the campaigns they conduct but very little control over which malware they use. An attribution analysis that considers only network level data would be inadequate against such an adversary.

Why do we perform cyber attribution, and who is the customer of cyber attribution decisions? Law enforcement and the courts care about cyber attribution decisions when making investigative or legal decisions. In other spheres, attribution decisions can be used to help determine the direction and proportion of an organizational response. For example, if a commercial company can determine if an attacker is part of an unsophisticated hacktivist gang rather than a sophisticated criminal enterprise, they could simply re-install the compromised computers as a defensive response rather than engaging with law enforcement. Likewise, according to Wheeler et al., "many offensive techniques, such as computer network attack, legal action (e.g., arrests and lawsuits), and kinetic energy attacks, can only be deployed if the source of the attack can be attributed with high confidence" [7].

© The Author(s) 2018
E. Nunes et al., *Artificial Intelligence Tools for Cyber Attribution*, SpringerBriefs in Computer Science, https://doi.org/10.1007/978-3-319-73788-1_1

In the spring of 2017, the internet was gripped by a widespread ransomware attack, dubbed WannaCry; the ransomware spread as a worm affecting 300,000 machines in 150 countries, holding files hostage with encryption and promising decryption if a payment was made to a Bitcoin address. Hackers took advantage of the fact that many systems were not updated with the patch released by Microsoft, leaving them vulnerable. The attack was in fact discussed on darkweb forums in several languages including English and Russian as identified by cybersecurity company CYR3CON [6]; they also reported that hackers choose medical institutions as prime targets based on the history of paid ransom from similar institutions. Both the distributed nature of the attack and the use of Bitcoin as payment obscure the true source and authorship of the worm. These features also limited the data available to perform attribution, because no central or hosted command and control systems were needed.

In this setting, the only artifacts available for attribution were the linguistic properties of the ransom message, and the code that made up the worm itself. An initial analysis and comparison of the ransomware code identified similarity in the code between WannaCry and malware that had previously been attributed to the "Lazarus Group." However, other explanations exist for this one point of similarity: perhaps the WannaCry authors borrowed from the Lazarus code after it was published; perhaps both authors copied from a third-party open source repository; perhaps this line was copied without the intent to deceive, because it is well known that developers will copy and paste code whenever possible.

Our research has focused on establishing a more rigorous and scientific basis for making attribution decisions. When the stakes are high, it is important to either make the correct decision, or understand the possibilities for deception and gather the additional information needed to make the correct decision. Having a single data point, as in the WannaCry example, could bias the analysis by giving too much weight to a single source.

In addition to researching and applying artificial intelligence tools to cyber attribution, we also ask: how do researchers train and evaluate these tools? Using data gathered from the real world is problematic for a few reasons. First, it is difficult to get real-world data due to the sensitive nature of the data. Additionally, even if the data were available, it is difficult to trust ground truth about that data. Could attackers' deceptions go unnoticed in this data? Who can say? To enable researchers to develop and evaluate their tools, we used data from capture-the-flag (CTF) contests, where access to the ground truth is available. We also present frameworks for executing and gathering your own CTF based data, while encouraging and monitoring attempts at deception.

In this book, we present the results of a research program that focuses on using artificial intelligence tools to enhance the cyber attribution process. In Chap. 2, we introduce a dataset collected from the capture-the-flag (CTF) event at DEFCON that has the identity of the attacker team (ground truth); the lack of such ground truth has limited previous studies to evaluate proposed models. As a first step, we use standard classification techniques to identify the attacker and summarize the results discussed in [1].

In Chap. 3, we propose a probabilistic structured argumentation framework that arises from the extension of Presumptive Defeasible Logic Programming (PreDeLP) with probabilistic models, and argue that this formalism is especially suitable for handling such contradictory and uncertain data. The framework has been demonstrated—via a case study—to handle cyber attribution [4].

In Chap. 4, we continue developing the DeLP3E model introduced in the previous chapter. We first propose a non-prioritized class of revision operators called **AFO** (Annotation Function-based Operators), and then go on to argue that in some cases it may be desirable to define revision operators that take quantitative aspects into account. As a result, we propose the **QAFO** (Quantitative Annotation Function-based Operators) class of operators, a subclass of **AFO**, and study the complexity of several problems related to their specification and application in revising knowledge bases. we present an algorithm for computing the probability that a literal is warranted in a DeLP3E knowledge base, and discuss how it could be applied towards implementing **QAFO**-style operators that compute approximations rather than exact operations [5].

In Chap. 5, we build argumentation models based on a formal reasoning framework called DeLP (Defeasible Logic Programming). The models are evaluated on the CTF data discussed in Chap. 2, comparing the performance of standard machine learning techniques with the proposed framework [2].

Finally, we discuss a capture-the-flag based framework to produce data with deception that can be used to evaluate proposed cyber attribution models—this framework is available as open source software [3].

References

1. E. Nunes, N. Kulkarni, P. Shakarian, A. Ruef, and J. Little. Cyber-deception and attribution in capture-the-flag exercises. In *Proceedings of the IEEE/ACM International Conference on Advances in Social Networks Analysis and Mining (ASONAM)*, pages 962–965. ACM, 2015.
2. E. Nunes, P. Shakarian, G. I. Simari, and A. Ruef. Argumentation models for cyber attribution. In *Proceedings of the IEEE/ACM International Conference on Advances in Social Networks Analysis and Mining (ASONAM)*, pages 837–844. IEEE, 2016.
3. A. Ruef, E. Nunes, P. Shakarian, and G. I. Simari. Measuring cyber attribution in games. In *Proceedings of the APWG Symposium on Electronic Crime Research (eCrime)*, pages 28–32, 2017.
4. P. Shakarian, G. I. Simari, G. Moores, D. Paulo, S. Parsons, M. A. Falappa, and A. Aleali. Belief revision in structured probabilistic argumentation. *Annals of Mathematics and Artificial Intelligence*, 78(3-4):259–301, 2016.
5. G. I. Simari, P. Shakarian, and M. A. Falappa. A quantitative approach to belief revision in structured probabilistic argumentation. *Annals of Mathematics and Artificial Intelligence*, 76(3-4):375–408, 2016.
6. J. Swarner. Before WannaCry was unleashed, hackers plotted about it on the Dark Web. 2017. Available at: http://www.slate.com/blogs/future_tense/2017/05/23/before_wannacry_was_unleashed_hackers_plotted_about_it_on_the_dark_web.html.
7. D. A. Wheeler and G. N. Larsen. Techniques for cyber attack attribution. Technical report, Institute for Defense Analyses, 2003.

Chapter 2
Baseline Cyber Attribution Models

2.1 Introduction

Attributing the culprit of a cyberattack is widely considered one of the major
technical and policy challenges of cybersecurity. Since the lack of ground truth
for an individual responsible for a given attack has limited previous studies, in
this chapter we take an important first step in developing computational techniques
toward attributing the actual culprit (here, a hacking group) responsible for a given
cyberattack. We leverage DEFCON capture-the-flag (CTF) exercise data that we
have processed to be amenable to various machine learning approaches. Here, we
use various classification techniques to identify the culprit in a cyberattack and
find that deceptive activities account for the majority of misclassified samples. We
also explore several heuristics to alleviate some of the misclassification caused by
deception. In this chapter, we:

- Assemble a dataset of cyberattacks with ground truth derived from the traffic of
  the CTF held at DEFCON 21 in 2013.
- Analyze this dataset to identify cyberattacks where deception occurred.
- Frame cyber attribution as a multi-label classification problem and leverage
  several machine learning approaches, finding that deceptive incidents account
  for the vast majority of misclassified samples.
- Introduce several pruning techniques and show that they can reduce the effect of
  deception, as well as provide insight into the conditions in which deception was
  employed by the participants of the CTF.

2.2 Dataset

In this section, we first describe the dataset and then go into the details of how we
processed it in order to make it amenable to analysis.

© The Author(s) 2018

E. Nunes et al., *Artificial Intelligence Tools for Cyber Attribution*, SpringerBriefs in
Computer Science, https://doi.org/10.1007/978-3-319-73788-1_2

2.2.1 DEFCON CTF

The DEFCON security conference sponsors and hosts a capture-the-flag (CTF) competition every year, held on site with the conference in Las Vegas, Nevada. DEFCON CTF is one of the oldest and best-known competitions—it has the highest average weight of all other CTF competitions on https://ctftime.org, which provides a ranking for CTF teams and CTF competitions.

CTF competitions can be categorized according to what role the competitors play in the competition: either *red team*, *blue team*, or a combination. In a blue team-focused CTF, the competitors harden their systems against a red team played by the organizers. In a combined red/blue team CTF, every team plays both blue and red team simultaneously. The NCCDC and CDX competitions are examples of a blue team CTF, while DEFCON CTF is a combined red/blue team. Each team is simultaneously responsible for hardening and defending their systems as well as identifying vulnerabilities and exploiting them in other teams' systems.

The game environment is created primarily by the DEFCON CTF organizers; the game focuses around programs (known in the game as *services*) written by them, which are engineered to contain specific vulnerabilities. The binary image of the service is made available to each team at the start of the game, but no other information about the service is released. Part of the challenge of the game is identifying the purpose of each service, as well as the vulnerabilities present in it. Identification of vulnerabilities serves both a defensive and offensive goal—once a vulnerability has been identified, a team may patch it in the binary program; additionally, the teams may create exploits for that vulnerability and use them to attack other teams and capture digital flags from their systems.

Each team is also provided with a server running the services, which contains the digital flags to be defended. To deter defensive actions such as powering off the server or stopping the services, the white team conducts periodic availability tests of the services running on each teams server. A team's score is the sum of the value of the flags they have captured, minus the sum of the flags that have been captured from that team, multiplied by an availability score determined by how often the white team was able to test that team's services. This scoring model incentivizes teams to keep their server online, identify the vulnerabilities in services and patch them quickly, and exploit other teams' services to capture their flags. On the other hand, it disincentivizes host-level blocking and shutting down services, as this would massively impact the final score.

This game environment can be viewed as a microcosm of the global Internet, and the careful game of "cat and mouse" between hacking groups and companies. Teams are free to use different technical means to discover vulnerabilities, such as *fuzzing* and reverse engineering on their own programs; alternatively, they may monitor the network data sent to their services and dynamically study the effects that network data has on unpatched services. If a team discovers a vulnerability and uses it against another team, the first team may discover that their exploit is re-purposed and used against them within minutes.

2.2.2 DEFCON CTF Data

The organizers of DEFCON CTF capture all of the network traffic sent and received by each team, and publish this data at the end of the competition [6]. This includes IP addresses for source and destination, as well as the full data sent and received (with timestamps). This data is not available to contestants in real time; depending on the organizers' choice from year to year, the contestants either have a real time feed but with the IP address obscured, or a full feed delivered on a time delay of minutes to hours. In addition to the traffic captures, copies of the vulnerable services are also distributed; though organizers usually do not disclose the vulnerabilities they engineered into each service, competitors frequently disclose this information publicly after the game is finished as technical write-ups.

The full interaction of all teams in the game environment is captured by this data. We cannot build a total picture of the game at any point in time, since there is state information from the servers that is not captured, but any exploit attempt would have to travel over the network and that would be observed in the data set.

2.2.3 Analysis of CTF Data

The CTF data set is very large, about 170 GB compressed; we used multiple systems with distributed and coordinated processing in our analysis of its contents. Fortunately, analyzing individual streams is an embarrassingly parallel task; we identified the TCP ports associated with each vulnerable service and, from this information, we used the open source tool tcpflow[1] to process the network captures into a set of files representing data sent or received on a particular connection.

This produced a corpus of data that could be searched and processed with standard UNIX tools, like grep. Further analysis of the game environment provided an indicator of when a data file contained an exploit. The game stored keys for services in a standard, hard-coded location on each competitors server. By searching for the text of this location in the data, we identified data files that contained exploits for services.

Once these data files were generated, we analyzed some of them by hand using the Interactive Disassembler (IDA) to determine if the data contained shell-code, which was indeed the case. We then used an automated tool to produce a summary of each data file as a JSON encoded element; included in this summary was a hash of the contents of the file and a histogram of the processor instructions contained therein. These JSON files were the final output of the low level analysis, transforming hundreds of gigabytes of network traffic into a manageable set of facts about exploit traffic in the data. Each JSON file is a list of tuples (time-stamp, hash, byte-histogram, instruction-histogram). These individual fields of the tuple are listed in Table 2.1.

---

[1] https://github.com/simsong/tcpflow.

Table 2.1 Fields in a single instance of a network attack

Field	Intuition
byte_hist	Histogram of byte sequences in the payload
inst_hist	Histogram of instructions used in the payload
from_team	The team where the payload originates (attacking team)
to_team	The team being attacked by the exploit
svc	The service that the payload is running
payload_hash	Indicates the payload used in the attack (md5)
time	Indicates the date and time of the attack

Table 2.2 Example event from the dataset

Field	Value
byte_hist	0×43:245, 0×69:8, $0 \times 3a$:9, $0 \times 5d$:1, ...
inst_hist	cmp:12, svcmi:2, subs:8, movtmi:60 ......
from_team	Men in black hats
to_team	Robot Mafia
svc	02345
payload_hash	2cc03b4e0053cde24400bbd80890446c
time	2013-08-03T23:45:17

This pre-processing of the network data (packets) yielded around 10 million network attacks. There are 20 teams in the CTF competition; in order to attribute an attack to a particular team, apart from analyzing the payloads used by the team, we also need to analyze the behavior of the attacking team towards their adversary. For this purpose we separated the network attacks according to the team being targeted; thus, we have 20 such subsets and we list them by team name in Table 2.3. An example of an event in the dataset is shown in Table 2.2.

We now discuss two important observations from the dataset, that makes the task of attributing a observed network attack to a team difficult.

Deception In the context of this dataset, we define an attack to be *deceptive* whenever multiple adversaries get mapped to a single attack pattern; therefore, in the current setting it refers to the scenario where the same exploit is used by multiple teams to target the same team. Figure 2.1 shows the distribution of unique deception attacks with respect to the total unique attacks in the dataset based on the target team. These unique deceptive attacks amount to just under 35% of the total unique attacks.

Duplicate Attacks A *duplicate* attack occurs when the same team uses the same payload to attack a team at different time instances. Duplicate attacks can be attributed to two reasons: first, when a team is trying to compromise another system, it does not just launch a single attack but rather a wave of attacks with very little time difference between consecutive attacks; second, once a successful payload is created that can penetrate the defense of other systems, it is used more by the original attacker as well as the deceptive one as compared to other payloads. We group

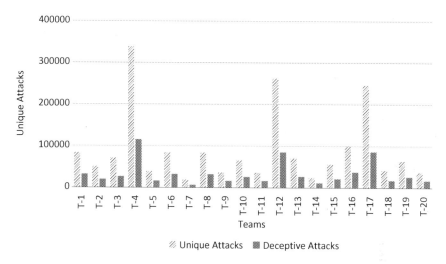

Fig. 2.1 Unique deceptive attacks directed towards each team

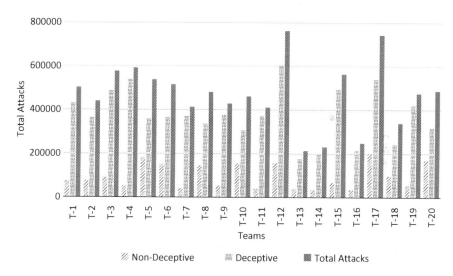

Fig. 2.2 Total attacks and duplicate attacks (both deceptive and non-deceptive) directed towards each team

duplicates as being either *non-deceptive* or *deceptive*. Non-deceptive duplicate are the duplicates of the team that first initiated the use of a particular payload; on the other hand, deceptive duplicates are all the attacks from the teams that are being deceptive. The latter form a large portion of the dataset, as seen in Fig. 2.2.

Analyzing the number of teams that use a particular payload, gives us insights into the deceptive behavior of teams. We plot the usage of unique payloads with respect to the number of teams using them in their attacks. We use four different categories namely payloads used by a single team, payloads used by two teams, payloads used by three teams and payloads used by more than three teams.

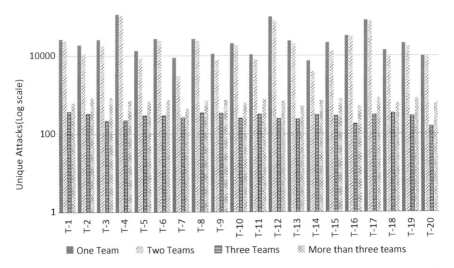

Fig. 2.3 Attacks on each target team carried out by one team, two teams, three teams, and more than three teams

Figure 2.3 shows the plot for each target team. A large fraction of unique payloads fall in the first two categories (one team and two teams).

2.3 Baseline Approaches

Since the data set contains all network information, in particular we have the ground truth (i.e., a team from Table 2.3) available for all the samples. Hence, we can use supervised machine learning approaches to predict the attacking team.

Decision Tree (DT) For baseline comparisons we first implemented a decision tree classifier—this hierarchical recursive partitioning algorithm is widely used for classification problems [3]. We built the decision tree by finding the attribute that maximizes information gain at each split. This attribute is termed as the *best split attribute*, and is used to split the node. The higher the information gain, the more pure the nodes that are split will be. During the testing phase, we check the test sample for the presence or absence of the best split attribute at each node until we reach the leaf node. The team that has the largest number of samples at the leaf node is predicted as the attack team for the test sample. In order to avoid over-fitting, we terminate the tree when the number of samples in the node is less than 0.1% of the training data.

Random Forest (RF) Random forest is an ensemble classification method proposed by Breiman [2]; it is based on the idea of generating multiple predictors that are then used in combination to classify unseen samples. The strength of the model lies in injecting randomness when building each classifier, and using random low dimensional subspaces to split the data at each node. We use a random forest

Table 2.3 Teams in the CTF competition

Notation	Team
T-1	9447
T-2	APT8
T-3	Alternatives
T-4	PPP
T-5	Robot Mafia
T-6	Samurai
T-7	The European Nopsled Team
T-8	WOWHacker-BIOS
T-9	[Technopandas]
T-10	Blue lotus
T-11	clgt
T-12	Men in black hats
T-13	More smoked leet chicken
T-14	pwnies
T-15	pwningyeti
T-16	Routards
T-17	raon_ASRT (whois)
T-18	Shell corp
T-19	shellphish
T-20	sutegoma2

that combines bagging [1] for each tree with random feature selection at each node to split the data, thus generating multiple decision tree classifiers. To split the data at each node we use information gain with random subspace projection, which indicates the amount of purity in the node with respect to class labels (more pure nodes result in higher information gain). Hence, we try to find the splits that maximize the information gain. The advantage of using a random forest over a single decision tree is low variance, and the notion that weak learners when combined together have a strong predictive power. During the test phase, each test sample gets a prediction from each individual decision tree (weak learner) giving its own opinion on test sample. The final decision is made by a majority vote among those trees.

Support Vector Machine (SVM) Support vector machines are a popular supervised classification technique proposed by Vapnik [5]; they work by finding a separating margin (a hyperplane) that maximizes the geometric distance between classes. We used the popular LibSVM implementation [4], which is publicly available. SVM is inherently a binary classifier, and it deals with multi-class classification problems by implementing several 1-vs-1 or 1-vs-all binary classifiers, which adds to the complexity as the number of classes increases.

Logistic Regression (LOG-REG) Logistic regression classifies samples by computing the odds ratio, which gives the strength of association between the features and the class. As opposed to linear regression, the output of logistic regression is the class probability of the sample belonging to that class. We implement the multinomial logistic regression, which handles multi-class classification.

2.4   Experimental Results

For our baseline experiments, we separate the attacks based on the team being targeted; thus, we have 20 attack datasets. We then sort the attack according to time, and reserve the first 90% of the attacks for training and the remaining 10% for testing. Attacker prediction accuracy is used as the performance measure for the experiment, which is defined as the fraction of correctly classified test samples. Figure 2.4 shows the accuracy for predicting the attacker for each target team; as we can see, machine learning techniques significantly outperform random guessing, which would have an average accuracy of choosing 1 out of 19 teams attacking (which on average would be correct only 5.3% of the time). For this experiment, the random forest classifier performs better than logistic regression, support vector machine, and decision tree for all the target teams. Table 2.4 summarizes the average performance for each method.

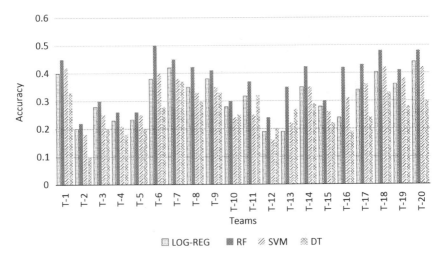

Fig. 2.4 Team prediction accuracy for LOG-REG, RF, SVM, and DT

Table 2.4 Summary of prediction results averaged across all teams

Method	Average performance
Decision tree (DT)	0.26
Logistic regression (LOG-REG)	0.31
Support vector machine (SVM)	0.30
Random forest (RF)	**0.37**

The bold value indicate the best performance of the model

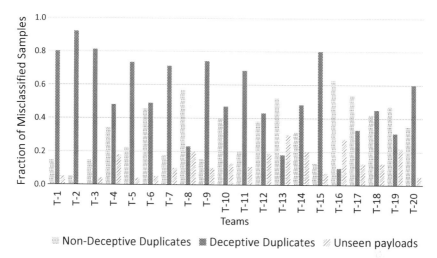

Fig. 2.5 Sources of error in the misclassified samples

2.4.1   Misclassified Samples

Misclassification can be attributed to the following sources,

- Non-deceptive duplicate attacks attributed to one of the deceptive teams.
- Deceptive duplicates attributed to some other deceptive team.
- Payloads that were not encountered during the training phase.

The first two sources of error make up the majority of misclassifications, since a given attack can be attributed to any of the 19 teams.

Figure 2.5 shows the distribution of the above-mentioned sources of misclassification for each team. Deceptive duplicates comprise the majority of misclassifications; this is not surprising, given the fact that deceptive duplicates make up almost 90% of the total attacks (see Fig. 2.2).

2.4.2   Pruning

We now explore different pruning techniques in order to address misclassification issues with respect to deceptive and non-deceptive duplicates. Pruning is only applied to the training data, while the test data is maintained at 10% as mentioned in Sect. 2.4; given that it is the best performer, we use the random forest classifier for all the pruning techniques. Our proposed pruning techniques are briefly described as follows:

- *All-but-majority:* Only consider the duplicates of the most attacking team given a payload, and prune other duplicates.

Table 2.5 Summary of prediction results averaged across all teams

Method	Average performance
Baseline approach (RF)	0.37
All-but-majority pruning (RF)	0.40
All-but-K-majority pruning (RF)	**0.42**
All-but-earliest pruning (RF)	0.34
All-but-most-recent pruning (RF)	0.36

The bold value indicate the best performance of the model

Table 2.6 Pruning technique performance comparison

Teams	RF	P-1(RF)	P-2(RF)	P-3(RF)	P-4(RF)
T-1	0.45	0.16	**0.46**	0.15	0.15
T-2	0.22	0.28	**0.30**	0.15	0.14
T-3	0.30	0.53	0.29	**0.57**	**0.57**
T-4	0.26	**0.33**	0.27	0.31	0.32
T-5	0.26	0.38	**0.45**	0.40	0.42
T-6	**0.50**	0.27	0.24	0.31	0.26
T-7	0.45	**0.59**	0.58	0.19	0.49
T-8	0.42	0.52	0.52	0.51	**0.55**
T-9	0.41	0.65	**0.68**	0.52	0.53
T-10	0.30	0.54	0.34	0.55	**0.57**
T-11	**0.37**	0.27	0.35	0.27	0.29
T-12	0.24	**0.37**	**0.37**	0.25	0.22
T-13	0.35	0.27	**0.37**	0.29	0.27
T-14	**0.42**	0.27	0.40	0.30	0.30
T-15	**0.30**	0.20	0.27	0.21	0.20
T-16	**0.42**	0.28	0.22	0.32	0.31
T-17	0.43	**0.45**	0.35	0.43	0.40
T-18	**0.48**	0.39	0.43	0.41	0.40
T-19	0.41	**0.65**	0.58	0.54	0.60
T-20	**0.48**	0.16	0.16	0.16	0.17

The bold values indicate the best performance of the model

- *All-but-K-majority:* Only consider the duplicates of the top *k* most frequent attacks given a payload, and prune the rest of the duplicates.
- *All-but-earliest-majority:* Retain the duplicates of the team that initiates the attack given a payload, while the rest of the duplicates are pruned.
- *All-but-most-recent-majority:* Retain the duplicates of the team that last used the payload in the training data, while the rest of the duplicates are pruned.

Table 2.5 gives the summary of the prediction results for all the pruning techniques in comparison with the random forest baseline approach; *All-but-K-majority* works best, with an average accuracy of 0.42.

All-But-Majority (P-1) In this pruning technique, for each payload we only retain duplicates of the most frequent attacking team and prune the duplicates of all other teams. This pruned set is then used to train the random forest classifier. Table 2.6 shows the classifier performance in comparison with the baseline method.

All-but-majority pruning has better performance on the test set than the baseline approach for 11 of the 20 teams. Using this pruning technique benefits the majority of the teams, as the prediction accuracy improves for them, but for some teams the performance drops. The reason for this drop in performance is due to the fact that the training set gets dominated by a single team that does not have a majority in the testing set. Since the majority team gets represented in most of the leaves of the random forest classifier, it gets predicted more often, leading to many misclassifications.

All-But-K-Majority (P-2) In order to address the issue of one team dominating in the training set, we use *all-but-K-majority*, where we consider the k most frequent teams for a payload under consideration. After trying out different values of k we select $k = 3$, which gives the best performance. For higher values of k, the pruning behaves like the baseline approach and for lower values it behaves like *All-but-majority*. On average, each team gains about $40,000$ samples in the training set as compared to *all-but-majority* pruning. Table 2.6 shows the classifier performance; in this case, pruning again performs better than baseline in 11 out of 20 teams, but as compared to *all-but-majority* the performance for most teams is better.

All-But-Earliest (P-3) In this kind of pruning we only retain the duplicates of the team that initiated the attack using a particular payload; this technique thus retains all the non-deceptive duplicates while getting rid of the deceptive ones. Table 2.6 shows the classifier performance; as we can see, it performs better than the baseline approach for 8 out of the 20 teams. Comparing this result to *all-but-majority* (including *all-but-K-majority*), it turns out that deceptive duplicates are informative in attributing an attack to a team, and should thus not be ignored completely.

All-But-Most-Recent (P-4) Here we repeat a similar procedure to *all-but-earliest*, but instead of retaining the duplicates of the team that initiated an attack, we retain the duplicates of the team that used the payload last in the training set. Since the data is sorted according to time, the last attacker becomes the most recent attacker for the test set. Table 2.6 shows the classifier performance.

2.5   Conclusions

In this chapter, we studied cyber attribution by examining DEFCON CTF data—this provided us with ground truth regarding the culprit responsible for each attack. We framed cyber attribution as a classification problem, and examined it using several machine learning approaches [7]. Our main finding was that deceptive incidents account for the vast majority of misclassified samples. We also went on to introduce heuristic pruning techniques that somewhat alleviate this problem. As we will see later on, more sophisticated techniques can significantly help push accuracy up.

References

1. L. Breiman. Bagging predictors. *Machine learning*, 24(2):123–140, 1996.
2. L. Breiman. Random forests. *Machine learning*, 45(1):5–32, 2001.
3. L. Breiman, J. Friedman, C. J. Stone, and R. A. Olshen. *Classification and regression trees*. CRC press, 1984.
4. C.-C. Chang and C.-J. Lin. Libsvm: A library for support vector machines. *ACM Transactions on Intelligent Systems and Technology (TIST)*, 2(3):27, 2011.
5. C. Cortes and V. Vapnik. Support vector networks. *Machine learning*, 20(3):273–297, 1995.
6. DEFCON. Capture the Flag. 2013. https://media.defcon.org/.
7. E. Nunes, N. Kulkarni, P. Shakarian, A. Ruef, and J. Little. Cyber-deception and attribution in capture-the-flag exercises. In *Proceedings of the IEEE/ACM International Conference on Advances in Social Networks Analysis and Mining (ASONAM)*, pages 962–965. ACM, 2015.

Chapter 3
Argumentation-Based Cyber Attribution: The **DeLP3E** Model

3.1 Introduction

In cyber-attribution, knowledge bases consisting of all the information that is available about a specific domain, along with all the available information about the current state of affairs, will typically contain contradictory data—that is because the knowledge base will have been constructed using data from different sources that disagree. We noted several examples of this for cyber-attribution in Chap. 2. This data will also, typically, contain some measure of uncertainty; thus, key problems that need to be addressed by formalisms for knowledge representation are the ability to handle contradictory information and to perform inference in the presence of uncertainty. These general problem aspects are very well suited for cyber attribution. We begin by providing a quick, motivating, sketch: the basic information in this scenario comes from a variety of different sources that only have a partial view of the domain, and since these sources disagree, having contradictory information in the knowledge base is unavoidable. In a cyberattack, it is not uncommon for the attacker to leave some false pieces of evidence with the goal of misleading the investigation, adding further contradictory information. Virtually none of the evidence that is gathered after an attack is conclusive, so there is uncertainty in the information that must be handled. Finally, since in responding to an attack new information is added to information that was gathered after previous attacks, it is necessary to update the knowledge base. In particular, if new information contradicts old information, it may be necessary to perform belief revision to recover consistency of some parts of the knowledge-base. However, we postpone the discussion of belief revision until Chap. 4, which is entirely devoted to this issue.

From this discussion we distill the requirements on any knowledge representation formalism that will be used in real-world cyber attribution applications. Such a formalism must be able to:

1. represent contradictory and uncertain information;

© The Author(s) 2018
E. Nunes et al., *Artificial Intelligence Tools for Cyber Attribution*, SpringerBriefs in Computer Science, https://doi.org/10.1007/978-3-319-73788-1_3

Table 3.1 Examples of the kind of information that could be represented in the environmental and analytical models in a cybersecurity application domain

Environmental model (EM)	Analytical model (AM)
Malware X was compiled on a system using the English language	Malware X was compiled on a system in English-speaking country Y
Country Y and country Z are currently at war	Country Y has a motive to launch a cyberattack against country Z
Malware W and malware X were created in a similar coding style	Malware W and malware X are related
Country Y has a significant investment in math-science-engineering (MSE) education	Country Y has the capability to conduct a cyberattack

2. answer queries on a knowledge base; and
3. handle revisions to the knowledge base.

This chapter presents a formalism called DeLP3E that meets all these requirements. A DeLP3E model consists of two parts, an *environmental model* (EM) and an *analytical model* (AM), which represent different aspects of a scenario. The idea is that the analytical model contains all the background information that is available for the analysis of the scenario. We envisage that this information is a combination of ontological information about the world; for instance (to take the old example), "*Tweety is a penguin*", "*penguins are birds*" and "*penguins do not fly*", and commonsense information that is relevant, for example "*birds generally fly*". As can be seen from this small example, the AM can be inconsistent, and so we will choose a formal model for the AM that can cope with inconsistency. On the other hand, the environmental model is intended to contain evidence that has been collected about a specific situation (an instance of the more general model in the AM) about which queries will be answered. In the classic example, "*Tweety is a penguin*" would be an element of the EM, but the EM can also be more subtle than this, allowing for the representation of uncertain information. If we did not know for sure that Tweety was a penguin, but just had some suggestive evidence that this is so, we could for example include in the EM the fact that "*Tweety is a penguin*" has a probability of 0.8 of being true. The EM is not limited to facts—we could also choose to model our evidence about Tweety with "*Tweety is a bird*" and "*Tweety is black and white*" and the rule that "*Black and white birds have a probability of 0.8 of being penguins*". A more complex pair of EM and AM, which relates to our motivating cybersecurity example, is given in Table 3.1.

The languages used in the AM and the EM are then related together though an *annotation function* (AF), which pairs formulas in the EM and the AM. Reasoning then consists of answering a query in the AM—when the AM is inconsistent this will involve establishing the relevant consistent subset to answer the query, computing the probability of the elements of the EM and, through the annotation function, establishing the probabilities that correspond to the answer to the initial query. Thus, in the Tweety example, to answer a query about whether Tweety can fly, the AM would reason about this truth or falsity of the proposition *"Tweety flies"*, the AF would identify which elements of the EM relate to this query, and the EM would provide a probability for these elements. The probability of the answer to the query, in this case either *"Tweety flies"* or *"Tweety does not fly"*, could then be computed. The inference of this probability is what we call *entailment*.

In our vision, DeLP3E is less a specific formalism and more a *family* of formalisms where different formal models for handling uncertainty can be used for the EM, and different logical reasoning models can be used for the AM. In this chapter, to make the discussion concrete, we make some specific choices. In particular, the EM is based on Nilsson's Probabilistic Logic [14], and the AM is based on the PreDeLP argumentation model from [13]. At the heart of PreDeLP is the notion of *presumptions*, elements of the knowledge base that can be presumed (assumed) to be true. This makes for a very natural connection to the EM—presumptions are elements of the AM that connect (through the annotation function) to elements of the EM, in the same way the other elements of the AM do. Thus, the presumptions will have a probability associated with them, and this is then used to establish the probability of the answer to the initial query.

This discussion has covered the requirement for DeLP3E to deal with inconsistency and uncertainty, and identified the need for inference. The final requirement is for the ability to revise the knowledge base, in particular the ability to perform belief revision in the sense of [1, 7, 8]. Given that belief revision is concerned with maintaining the consistency of a set of beliefs and that DeLP3E is built around an argumentation system that can handle inconsistency, at first glance it might not be obvious why belief revision is required. However, after some reflection it becomes clear that all three parts of a DeLP3E model—the environmental model, the analytical model, and the annotation function—may require revision, at least in the instantiation of DeLP3E that we consider here. The EM is underpinned by probability theory, and this places the constraint that the set of propositions used in the EM be consistent (a constraint that would not necessarily exist if we were to use a different uncertainty handling mechanism). The AM is built using PreDeLP, and though there can be inconsistency in some elements of a PreDeLP model, the strict rules and facts used to answer a specific query must be consistent, and so belief revision is required (if we built the AM using an argumentation system that only included defeasible knowledge, as in [16], belief revision would not be required). Finally, though there is never a strict requirement for belief revision of the AF, as we will discuss in Chap. 4, providing the ability to revise the annotation function can help us to avoid revising other aspects of the model.

3.1.1 Application to the Cyber Attribution Problem

AS we have already discussed in previous chapters, cyber attribution—the problem of determining who was responsible for a given cyberoperation, be it an incident of attack, reconnaissance, or information theft [19]—is an important issue. The difficulty of this problem stems not only from the amount of effort required to find forensic clues, but also the ease with which an attacker can plant false clues to mislead security personnel. Further, while techniques such as forensics and reverse-engineering [2], source tracking [25], honeypots [23], and sinkholing [17] are commonly employed to find evidence that can lead to attribution, it is unclear how this evidence is to be combined and reasoned about. In some cases, such evidence is augmented with normal intelligence collection, such as human intelligence (HUMINT), signals intelligence (SIGINT) and other means—this adds additional complications to the task of attributing a given operation.

In essence, cyber attribution is a highly-technical intelligence analysis problem where an analyst must consider a variety of sources, each with its associated level of confidence, to provide a decision maker (e.g., a system administrator or Chief Information Officer) with insight into who conducted a given operation. Indeed, while previous cyber attribution approaches only consider a single source of information, our approach takes into account multiple sources of information due to its ability to deal with inconsistency. As it is well-known that people's ability to conduct intelligence analysis is limited [9], and due to the highly technical nature of many cyber evidence-gathering techniques, an automated reasoning system would be best suited for the task. Such a system must be able to accomplish several goals:

- Reason about evidence in a formal, principled manner, i.e., relying on strong computational and mathematical foundations.
- Consider evidence for cyber attribution associated with some level of uncertainty (expressed via probabilities).
- Consider logical rules that allow for the system to draw conclusions based on certain pieces of evidence and iteratively apply such rules.
- Consider pieces of information that may not be compatible with each other, decide which information is most relevant, and express why.
- Attribute a given cyberoperation based on the above-described features and provide the analyst with the ability to understand how the system arrived at that conclusion.

The fit between these requirements and the abilities of DeLP3E led us to develop a use case based around cyber attribution[1] as a way of showcasing the functionality of DeLP3E. This use case is described in detail in Sect. 3.5.

3.1.2 Structure of the Chapter

The structure of the chapter broadly follows the first two of the requirements identified above. First, in Sect. 3.2 we introduce the environmental and analytical model, where the environmental model makes use of Nilsson's probabilistic

---

[1]The causality is a little more complicated than this sentence suggests. The cyber attribution problem was indeed the original motivation for the development of DeLP3E, and elements of the example evolved along with the formalism.

logic [14] and the analytical model builds upon PreDeLP [13]. The resulting framework is the general-purpose probabilistic argumentation language DeLP3E, which stands for *Defeasible Logic Programming with Presumptions and Probabilistic Environment*. This is formally laid out in Sect. 3.3, which also studies the entailment problem for DeLP3E. Finally, Sect. 3.5 then presents a use case of DeLP3E in the context of cyber attribution.

3.2 Technical Preliminaries

This section presents the two main building blocks of the DeLP3E framework: the environmental model and the analytical model.

3.2.1 Basic Language

We assume sets of variables and constants, denoted with **V** and **C**, respectively. In the rest of this chapter, we will follow the convention from the logic programming literature and use capital letters to represent variables (e.g., X, Y, Z) and lowercase letters to represent constants.

The next component of the language is a set of predicate symbols. Each predicate symbol has an arity bounded by a constant value; the EM and AM use separate sets of predicate symbols, denoted with $\mathbf{P}_{EM}, \mathbf{P}_{AM}$, respectively—the two models can, however, share variables and constants.

As usual, a *term* is composed of either a variable or a constant. Given terms $t_1, \ldots, t_n$ and n-ary predicate symbol p, $p(t_1, \ldots, t_n)$ is called an *atom*; if $t_1, \ldots, t_n$ are constants, then the atom is said to be *ground*. The sets of all ground atoms for the EM and AM are denoted with $\mathbf{G}_{EM}$ and $\mathbf{G}_{AM}$, respectively.

Given a set of ground atoms, a *world* is any subset of atoms—those that belong to the set are said to be *true* in the world, while those that do not are *false*. Therefore, there are $2^{|\mathbf{G}_{EM}|}$ possible worlds in the EM and $2^{|\mathbf{G}_{AM}|}$ worlds in the AM; these sets are denoted with $\mathcal{W}_{EM}$ and $\mathcal{W}_{AM}$, respectively. In order to avoid worlds that do not model possible situations given a particular domain, we include *integrity constraints* of the form $\mathsf{oneOf}(\mathscr{A}')$, where $\mathscr{A}'$ is a subset of ground atoms. Intuitively, such a constraint states that any world where more than one of the atoms from set $\mathscr{A}'$ appears is invalid. We use $\mathbf{IC}_{EM}$ and $\mathbf{IC}_{AM}$ to denote the sets of integrity constraints for the EM and AM, respectively, and the sets of worlds that conform to these constraints is denoted with $\mathcal{W}_{EM}(\mathbf{IC}_{EM})$ and $\mathcal{W}_{AM}(\mathbf{IC}_{AM})$, respectively.

Finally, logical formulas arise from the combination of atoms using the traditional connectives ($\land$, $\lor$, and $\neg$). As usual, we say that a world w *satisfies* formula f, written $w \models f$, iff: (i) If f is an atom, then $w \models f$ iff $f \in w$; (ii) if $f = \neg f'$ then $w \models f$ iff $w \not\models f'$; (iii) if $f = f' \land f''$ then $w \models f$ iff $w \models f'$ and $w \models f''$; and (iv) if $f = f' \lor f''$ then $w \models f$ iff $w \models f'$ or $w \models f''$. We use the notation $form_{EM}, form_{AM}$ to denote the set of all possible (ground) formulas in the EM and AM, respectively.

Example 3.1 Thus, the following are terms

$a \quad b \quad c \quad d \quad e \quad f \quad p(X)$
$g \quad h \quad i \quad j \quad k \quad p(a)$

and the following are formulas using those terms:

$a \quad d \wedge e \qquad k$
$b \quad f \wedge g \wedge h$
$c \quad i \vee \neg j$

∎

3.2.2   Environmental Model

The EM is used to describe the probabilistic knowledge that we have about the domain. In general, the EM contains knowledge such as evidence, uncertain facts, or knowledge about agents and systems. Here we base the EM on the probabilistic logic of [14], which we now briefly review.

Definition 3.1 Let f be a formula over $\mathbf{P}_{EM}$, $\mathbf{V}$, and $\mathbf{C}$, $p \in [0, 1]$, and $\epsilon \in [0, \min(p, 1 - p)]$. A *probabilistic formula* is of the form $f : p \pm \epsilon$. A set $\mathcal{K}_{EM}$ of probabilistic formulas is called a *probabilistic knowledge base*.

In the above definition, the number ϵ is referred to as an *error tolerance*. Intuitively, the probabilistic formula $f : p \pm \epsilon$ is interpreted as "formula f is true with probability between $p - \epsilon$ and $p + \epsilon$". Note that there are no further constraints over this interval apart from those imposed by other probabilistic formulas in the knowledge base. The uncertainty regarding the probability values stems from the fact that certain assumptions (such as probabilistic independence between all formulas) may not hold in the environment being modeled.

Example 3.2   Consider the following set $\mathcal{K}_{EM}$:

$f_1 = a : 0.7 \pm 0.2 \quad f_4 = d \wedge e \quad : 0.8 \pm 0.1 \quad f_7 = k \quad : 1 \pm 0$
$f_2 = b : 0.3 \pm 0.1 \quad f_5 = f \wedge g \wedge h : 0.5 \pm 0.1 \quad f_8 = a \wedge b : 0.3 \pm 0.1$
$f_3 = c : 0.6 \pm 0.2 \quad f_6 = i \vee \neg j \quad : 0.8 \pm 0.2$

Throughout the chapter, we also use $\mathcal{K}'_{EM} = \{f_1, f_2, f_3\}$ ∎

A set of probabilistic formulas describes a set of possible probability distributions Pr over the set $\mathcal{W}_{EM}(\mathbf{IC}_{EM})$. We say that probability distribution Pr *satisfies* probabilistic formula $f : p \pm \epsilon$ iff:

$$p - \epsilon \leq \sum_{w \in \mathcal{W}_{EM}(\mathbf{IC}_{EM}), w \models f} Pr(w) \leq p + \epsilon.$$

A probability distribution over $\mathcal{W}_{EM}(\mathbf{IC}_{EM})$ *satisfies* $\mathcal{K}_{EM}$ iff it satisfies all probabilistic formulas in $\mathcal{K}_{EM}$.

Given a probabilistic knowledge base and a (non-probabilistic) formula q, the *maximum entailment* problem seeks to identify real numbers p, ϵ such that all valid probability distributions Pr that satisfy $\mathcal{K}_{EM}$ also satisfy $q : p \pm \epsilon$, and there does not exist p', ϵ' s.t. $[p-\epsilon, p+\epsilon] \supset [p'-\epsilon', p'+\epsilon']$, where all probability distributions Pr that satisfy $\mathcal{K}_{EM}$ also satisfy $q : p' \pm \epsilon'$. In order to solve this problem we must solve the linear program defined below.

Definition 3.2 Given a knowledge base $\mathcal{K}_{EM}$ and a formula q, we have a variable x_i for each $w_i \in \mathcal{W}_{EM}(\mathbf{IC}_{EM})$. Each variable x_i corresponds with the probability of w_i occurring.

- For each $f_j : p_j \pm \epsilon_j \in \mathcal{K}_{EM}$, there is a constraint of the form:

$$p_j - \epsilon_j \leq \sum_{w_i \in \mathcal{W}_{EM}(\mathbf{IC}_{EM}) s.t. \ w_i \models f_j} x_i \leq p_j + \epsilon_j.$$

- We also have the constraint:

$$\sum_{w_i \in \mathcal{W}_{EM}(\mathbf{IC}_{EM})} x_i = 1.$$

- The objective is to minimize the function:

$$\sum_{w_i \in \mathcal{W}_{EM}(\mathbf{IC}_{EM}) s.t. \ w_i \models q} x_i.$$

We use the notation EP-LP-MIN($\mathcal{K}_{EM}, q$) to refer to the value of the objective function in the solution to the EM-LP-MIN constraints.

The next step is to solve the linear program a second time, but this time maximizing the objective function (we shall refer to this as EM-LP-MAX)—let ℓ and u be the results of these operations, respectively. In [14], it is shown that:

$$\epsilon = \frac{u - \ell}{2} \text{ and } p = \ell + \epsilon$$

is the solution to the maximum entailment problem. We note that although the above linear program has an exponential number of variables in the worst case (i.e., no integrity constraints), the presence of constraints has the potential to greatly reduce this space. Further, there are also good heuristics (cf. [10, 22]) that have been shown to provide highly accurate approximations with a reduced-size linear program.

Example 3.3 Consider KB $\mathcal{K}'_{EM}$ from Example 3.2 and a set of ground atoms restricted to those that appear in that program; we have the following worlds:

$$w_1 = \{a, b, c\} \quad w_2 = \{a, b\} \quad w_3 = \{a, c\} \quad w_4 = \{b, c\}$$
$$w_5 = \{b\} \quad\quad w_6 = \{a\} \quad\quad w_7 = \{c\} \quad\quad w_8 = \emptyset$$

and suppose we wish to compute the probability for formula $q = a \vee c$.

For each formula in $\mathscr{K}_{EM}$ we have a constraint, and for each world above we have a variable. An objective function is created based on the worlds that satisfy the query formula (in this case, worlds $w_1, w_2, w_3, w_4, w_6, w_7$). Solving EP-LP-MAX($\mathscr{K}'_{EM}, q$) and EP-LP-MIN($\mathscr{K}'_{EM}, q$), we obtain the solution 0.9 ± 0.1. Thus, the former can be written as follows:

$$
\begin{array}{llll}
\max & x_1 + x_2 + x_3 + x_4 + x_6 + x_7 & w.r.t. : \\
0.6 \leq & x_1 + x_2 + x_3 + x_6 & \leq 0.8 \\
0.2 \leq & x_1 + x_2 + x_4 + x_5 & \leq 0.4 \\
0.8 \leq & x_1 + x_3 + x_4 + x_7 & \leq 1 \\
& x_1 + x_2 + x_3 + x_4 + x_5 + x_6 + x_7 + x_8 = 1
\end{array}
$$

From this, we can solve EP-LP-MAX($\mathscr{K}'_{EM}, q$) and, after an easy modification, EP-LP-MIN($\mathscr{K}'_{EM}, q$), and obtain the solution 0.9 ± 0.1.   ∎

3.2.3 Analytical Model

The analytical model contains information that a user may conclude based on the information in the environmental model. While the EM contains information that can have probabilities associated with it, statements in the AM can be either true or false depending on a certain combination (or several possible combinations) of statements from the EM.

For the AM, we choose to represent information using a structured argumentation framework [15] since this kind of formalism meets the representational requirements discussed in the introduction. Unlike the EM, which describes probabilistic information about the state of the real world, the AM must allow for competing ideas. Therefore, it must be able to represent contradictory information. The algorithmic approach we shall later describe allows for the creation of *arguments* based on the AM that may "compete" with each other to answer a given query. In this competition—known as a *dialectical process*—one argument may defeat another based on a *comparison criterion* that determines the prevailing argument. Resulting from this process, certain arguments are *warranted* (those that are not *defeated* by other arguments), thereby providing a suitable explanation for the answer to a given query.

The transparency provided by the system can allow knowledge engineers and users of the system to identify potentially incorrect input information and fine-tune the models or, alternatively, collect more information. In short, argumentation-based reasoning has been studied as a natural way to manage a set of inconsistent information—it is the way humans settle disputes. As we will see, another desirable characteristic of (structured) argumentation frameworks is that, once a conclusion is reached, we are left with an explanation of *how we arrived at it* and information about why a given argument is warranted; this is very important information for users to have.

The formal model that we use for the AM is Defeasible Logic Programming with Presumptions (PreDeLP) [13], a formalism combining logic programming with defeasible argumentation. Here, we briefly recall the basics of PreDeLP—we refer the reader to [6, 13] for the complete presentation. Formally, we use the notation

$$\Pi_{AM} = (\Theta, \Omega, \Phi, \Delta)$$

to denote a PreDeLP program, where Ω is a set of strict rules, Θ is a set of facts, Δ is a set of defeasible rules, and Φ is a set of presumptions. We now define these constructs formally.

Facts (Θ) are ground literals representing atomic information or its negation, using strong negation "$\neg$". Note that all of the literals in our framework must be formed with a predicate from the set $\mathbf{P}_{AM}$. Note that information in the form of facts cannot be contradicted. We will use the notation $[\Theta]$ to denote the set of all possible facts.

Strict Rules (Ω) represent non-defeasible cause-and-effect information that resembles an implication (though the semantics is different since the contrapositive does not hold) and are of the form $L_0 \leftarrow L_1, \ldots, L_n$, where L_0 is a ground literal and $\{L_i\}_{i>0}$ is a set of ground literals. We will use the notation $[\Omega]$ to denote the set of all possible strict rules.

Presumptions (Φ) are ground literals of the same form as facts, except that they are not taken as being true but rather are defeasible, which means that they can be contradicted. Presumptions are denoted in the same manner as facts, except that the symbol $\prec$ is added. We note that, epistemologically, presumptions cannot be treated as special cases of defeasible rules; intuitively, this is because unless further criteria are applied, an argument that uses a set of presumptions should be defeated by arguments that use a subset of them, and this would not necessarily be the case if presumptions were expressed as defeasible rules. The treatment of presumptions in this manner also necessitates an extension to generalized specificity; we refer the interested reader to [13] for further details.

Defeasible Rules (Δ) represent tentative knowledge that can be used if nothing can be posed against it. Just as presumptions are the defeasible counterpart of facts, defeasible rules are the defeasible counterpart of strict rules. They are of the form $L_0 \prec L_1, \ldots, L_n$, where L_0 is a ground literal and $\{L_i\}_{i>0}$ is a set of ground literals. In both strict and defeasible rules, *strong negation* is allowed in the head of rules, and hence may be used to represent contradictory knowledge.

Even though the above constructs are ground, we allow for schematic versions with variables that are used to represent sets of ground rules. In Fig. 3.1, we provide an example Π_{AM} of a ground knowledge base. (Figure 3.7 gives an example of a non-ground knowledge base.)

Arguments Given a query in the form of a ground atom, the goal is to derive arguments for and against its validity—derivation follows the mechanism of logic programming [12]. Since rule heads can contain strong negation, it is possible to defeasibly derive contradictory literals from a program. For the treatment of contradictory knowledge, PreDeLP incorporates a defeasible argumentation

$$\Theta : \theta_{1a} = p \qquad \theta_{1b} = q \qquad\qquad \theta_2 = r$$

$$\Omega : \omega_{1a} = \neg s \leftarrow t \quad \omega_{2a} = s \leftarrow p,u,r,v$$
$$\omega_{1b} = \neg t \leftarrow s \quad \omega_{2b} = t \leftarrow q,w,x,v$$

$$\Phi : \phi_1 = \ y \prec \qquad \phi_2 = \ v \prec \qquad\qquad \phi_3 = \ \neg z \prec$$

$$\Delta : \delta_{1a} = s \prec p \quad \delta_2 = \ s \prec u \quad\quad \delta_{5a} = \neg u \prec \neg z$$
$$\delta_{1b} = t \prec q \quad \delta_3 = \ s \prec r,v \quad \delta_{5b} = \neg w \prec \neg n$$
$$\delta_4 = \ u \prec y$$

Fig. 3.1 A ground argumentation framework

formalism that allows the identification of the pieces of knowledge that are in conflict and, through the previously mentioned dialectical process, decides which information prevails as warranted. This dialectical process involves the construction and evaluation of arguments, building a *dialectical tree* in the process. Arguments are formally defined next.

Definition 3.3 An *argument* $\langle \mathscr{A}, L \rangle$ for a literal L is a pair of the literal and a (possibly empty) set of the AM ($\mathscr{A} \subseteq \Pi_{AM}$) that provides a minimal proof for L meeting the following requirements: (i) L is defeasibly derived from $\mathscr{A}$; (ii) $\Omega \cup \Theta \cup \mathscr{A}$ is not contradictory; and (iii) $\mathscr{A}$ is a minimal subset of $\Delta \cup \Phi$.

Literal L is called the *conclusion* supported by the argument, and $\mathscr{A}$ is the *support* of the argument. An argument $\langle \mathscr{B}, L \rangle$ is a *subargument* of $\langle \mathscr{A}, L' \rangle$ iff $\mathscr{B} \subseteq \mathscr{A}$. An argument $\langle \mathscr{A}, L \rangle$ is *presumptive* iff $\mathscr{A} \cap \Phi$ is not empty. We will also use $\Omega(\mathscr{A}) = \mathscr{A} \cap \Omega$, $\Theta(\mathscr{A}) = \mathscr{A} \cap \Theta$, $\Delta(\mathscr{A}) = \mathscr{A} \cap \Delta$, and $\Phi(\mathscr{A}) = \mathscr{A} \cap \Phi$. For convenience, we may sometimes call an argument by its support. (e.g. argument $\mathscr{A}$ instead of argument $\langle \mathscr{A}, L \rangle$.)

Our definition differs slightly from that of [21], where DeLP is introduced, as we include strict rules and facts as part of arguments—this is due to the fact that in our framework, the components of an argument can only be used in certain environmental conditions. Hence, a fact may be true in one EM world and not another. This causes us to include facts and strict rules as part of the argument. We discuss this further in Sect. 3.3 (page 30).

Definition 3.4 A literal is derived from an argument if it appears as a fact or a presumption in the argument or appears in the head of a strict rule or a defeasible rule where all the literals in the body of that strict rule or defeasible rule are derived from that argument.

Example 3.4 Figure 3.2 shows example arguments based on the knowledge base from Fig. 3.1. Note that $\langle \mathscr{A}_5, u \rangle$ is a sub-argument of $\langle \mathscr{A}_2, s \rangle$ and $\langle \mathscr{A}_3, s \rangle$. ∎

Given an argument $\langle \mathscr{A}_1, L_1 \rangle$, counter-arguments are arguments that contradict it. Argument $\langle \mathscr{A}_1, L_1 \rangle$ is said to *counterargue* or *attack* $\langle \mathscr{A}_2, L_2 \rangle$ at a literal L' iff there exists a subargument $\langle \mathscr{A}, L' \rangle$ of $\langle \mathscr{A}_2, L_2 \rangle$ such that the set $\Omega(\mathscr{A}_1) \cup \Omega(\mathscr{A}_2) \cup \Theta(\mathscr{A}_1) \cup \Theta(\mathscr{A}_2) \cup \{L_1, L'\}$ is inconsistent.

$$
\begin{array}{ll}
\langle \mathscr{A}_1, s\rangle & \mathscr{A}_1 = \{\theta_{1a}, \delta_{1a}\} \qquad \langle \mathscr{A}_2, s\rangle \quad \mathscr{A}_2 = \{\phi_1, \phi_2, \delta_4, \omega_{2a}, \theta_{1a}, \theta_2\} \\
\langle \mathscr{A}_3, s\rangle & \mathscr{A}_3 = \{\phi_1, \delta_2, \delta_4\} \qquad \langle \mathscr{A}_4, s\rangle \quad \mathscr{A}_4 = \{\phi_2, \delta_3, \theta_2\} \\
\langle \mathscr{A}_5, u\rangle & \mathscr{A}_5 = \{\phi_1, \delta_4\} \qquad\quad \langle \mathscr{A}_6, \neg s\rangle \;\, \mathscr{A}_6 = \{\delta_{1b}, \theta_{1b}, \omega_{1a}\} \\
\langle \mathscr{A}_7, \neg u\rangle & \mathscr{A}_7 = \{\phi_3, \delta_{5a}\}
\end{array}
$$

Fig. 3.2 Example ground arguments from the framework of Fig. 3.1

Example 3.5 Consider the arguments from Example 3.4. The following are some of the attack relationships between them: $\mathscr{A}_1$, $\mathscr{A}_2$, $\mathscr{A}_3$, and $\mathscr{A}_4$ all attack $\mathscr{A}_6$; $\mathscr{A}_5$ attacks $\mathscr{A}_7$; and $\mathscr{A}_7$ attacks $\mathscr{A}_2$. ∎

A *proper defeater* of an argument $\langle A, L\rangle$ is a counter-argument that—by some criterion—is considered to be better than $\langle A, L\rangle$; if the two are incomparable according to this criterion, the counterargument is said to be a *blocking* defeater. An important characteristic of PreDeLP is that the argument comparison criterion is modular, and thus the most appropriate criterion for the domain that is being represented can be selected; the default criterion used in classical defeasible logic programming (from which PreDeLP is derived) is *generalized specificity* [24], though an extension of this criterion is required for arguments using presumptions [13]. We briefly recall this criterion next—the first definition is for generalized specificity, which is subsequently used in the definition of presumption-enabled specificity.

Definition 3.5 (Generalized Specificity) Let $\Pi_{AM} = (\Theta, \Omega, \Phi, \Delta)$ be a PreDeLP program and let $\mathscr{F}$ be the set of all literals that have a defeasible derivation from Π_{AM}. An argument $\langle \mathscr{A}_1, L_1\rangle$ is *preferred* to $\langle \mathscr{A}_2, L_2\rangle$, denoted with $\mathscr{A}_1 \succ_{PS} \mathscr{A}_2$ iff the two following conditions hold:

(1) For all $H \subseteq \mathscr{F}$, $\Omega \cup H$ is non-contradictory: if there is a derivation for L_1 from $\Omega \cup H \cup DR(\mathscr{A}_1)$, and there is no derivation for L_1 from $\Omega \cup H$, then there is a derivation for L_2 from $\Omega \cup H \cup DR(\mathscr{A}_2)$.

(2) There is at least one set $H' \subseteq \mathscr{F}$, $\Omega \cup H'$ is non-contradictory, such that there is a derivation for L_2 from $\Omega \cup H' \cup DR(\mathscr{A}_2)$, there is no derivation for L_2 from $\Omega \cup H'$, and there is no derivation for L_1 from $\Omega \cup H \cup DR(\mathscr{A}_1)$.

Intuitively, the principle of specificity says that, in the presence of two conflicting lines of argument about a proposition, the one that uses more of the available information is more convincing. Returning to the Tweety example: there are arguments stating both that Tweety flies (because it is a bird) and that Tweety doesn't fly (because it is a penguin). The latter uses more information about Tweety—it is more specific because it is information that Tweety is not just a bird, but is a penguin-bird, the subset of birds that are penguins—and is thus the stronger of the two.

Definition 3.6 (Presumption-Enabled Specificity [13]) Given PreDeLP program $\Pi_{AM} = (\Theta, \Omega, \Phi, \Delta)$, an argument $\langle \mathscr{A}_1, L_1\rangle$ is *preferred* to $\langle \mathscr{A}_2, L_2\rangle$, denoted with $\mathscr{A}_1 \succ \mathscr{A}_2$ iff any of the following conditions hold:

(1) $\langle \mathscr{A}_1, L_1 \rangle$ and $\langle \mathscr{A}_2, L_2 \rangle$ are both factual, which is an argument using none of the presumptions or defeasible rules and $\langle \mathscr{A}_1, L_1 \rangle \succ_{PS} \langle \mathscr{A}_2, L_2 \rangle$.
(2) $\langle \mathscr{A}_1, L_1 \rangle$ is a factual argument and $\langle \mathscr{A}_2, L_2 \rangle$ is a presumptive argument, which is an argument using at least one of the presumptions or defeasible rules.
(3) $\langle \mathscr{A}_1, L_1 \rangle$ and $\langle \mathscr{A}_2, L_2 \rangle$ are presumptive arguments, and

    (a) $\Phi(\mathscr{A}_1) \subsetneq \Phi(\mathscr{A}_2)$ or,
    (b) $\Phi(\mathscr{A}_1) = \Phi(\mathscr{A}_2)$ and $\langle \mathscr{A}_1, L_1 \rangle \succ_{PS} \langle \mathscr{A}_2, L_2 \rangle$.

Generally, if $\mathscr{A}$ and $\mathscr{B}$ are arguments with rules X and Y, respectively and $X \subset Y$, then $\mathscr{A}$ is stronger than $\mathscr{B}$. This also holds when $\mathscr{A}$ and $\mathscr{B}$ use presumptions P_1 and P_2, resp., and $P_1 \subset P_2$.

Example 3.6 The following are some relationships between arguments from Example 3.4, based on Definitions 3.5 and 3.6:

- $\mathscr{A}_1$ and $\mathscr{A}_6$ are incomparable (blocking defeaters);
- $\mathscr{A}_6 \succ \mathscr{A}_2$, and thus $\mathscr{A}_6$ defeats $\mathscr{A}_2$;
- $\mathscr{A}_5$ and $\mathscr{A}_7$ are incomparable (blocking defeaters).   ■

A sequence of arguments called an *argumentation line* thus arises from this attack relation, where each argument defeats its predecessor. To avoid undesirable sequences, which may represent circular argumentation lines, in DeLP an *argumentation line* is *acceptable* if it satisfies certain constraints (see below). A literal L is *warranted* if there exists a non-defeated argument $\mathscr{A}$ supporting L.

Definition 3.7 (Adapted from [6]) Let $\Pi_{AM} = (\Theta, \Omega, \Phi, \Delta)$ be a PreDeLP program. Two arguments $\langle \mathscr{A}_1, L_1 \rangle$ and $\langle \mathscr{A}_2, L_2 \rangle$ are *concordant* iff the set $\mathscr{A}_1 \cup \mathscr{A}_2$ is non-contradictory.

Definition 3.8 ([6]) Let Λ be an argumentation line. Λ is an *acceptable argumentation line* iff:

(1) Λ is a finite sequence.
(2) The set Λ_S, of supporting arguments is concordant, and the set Λ_I of interfering arguments is concordant.
(3) No argument $\langle \mathscr{A}_k, L_k \rangle$ in Λ is a subargument of an argument $\langle \mathscr{A}_i, L_i \rangle$ appearing earlier in Λ ($i < k$)
(4) For all i, such that the argument $\langle \mathscr{A}_i, K_i \rangle$ is a blocking defeater for $\langle A_{i-1}, \mathscr{K}_{i-1} \rangle$, if $\langle A_{i+1}, \mathscr{K}_{i+1} \rangle$ exists, then $\langle A_{i+1}, \mathscr{K}_{i+1} \rangle$ is a proper defeater for $\langle A_i, \mathscr{K}_i \rangle$.

Clearly, there can be more than one defeater for a particular argument $\langle \mathscr{A}, L \rangle$. Therefore, many acceptable argumentation lines could arise from $\langle \mathscr{A}, L \rangle$, leading to a tree structure. The tree is built from the set of all argumentation lines rooted in the initial argument. In a dialectical tree, every node (except the root) represents a defeater of its parent, and leaves correspond to undefeated arguments. Each path from the root to a leaf corresponds to a different acceptable argumentation line. A dialectical tree provides a structure for considering all the possible acceptable argumentation lines that can be generated for deciding whether an argument is defeated. This tree is called *dialectical* because it represents an exhaustive dialectical[2] analysis for the argument in its root. For a given argument $\langle \mathscr{A}, L \rangle$, we denote the corresponding dialectical tree as $\mathscr{T}(\langle \mathscr{A}, L \rangle)$.

Given a literal L and an argument $\langle \mathscr{A}, L \rangle$, in order to decide whether or not a literal L is warranted, every node in the dialectical tree $\mathscr{T}(\langle \mathscr{A}, L \rangle)$ is recursively marked as "D" (*defeated*) or "U" (*undefeated*), obtaining a marked dialectical tree $\mathscr{T}^*(\langle \mathscr{A}, L \rangle)$ as follows:

1. All leaves in $\mathscr{T}^*(\langle \mathscr{A}, L \rangle)$ are marked as "U" s, and
2. Let $\langle \mathscr{B}, q \rangle$ be an inner node of $\mathscr{T}^*(\langle \mathscr{A}, L \rangle)$. Then $\langle \mathscr{B}, q \rangle$ will be marked as "U" iff every child of $\langle \mathscr{B}, q \rangle$ is marked as "D". The node $\langle \mathscr{B}, q \rangle$ will be marked as "D" iff it has at least a child marked as "U".

Given an argument $\langle \mathscr{A}, L \rangle$ obtained from Π_{AM}, if the root of $\mathscr{T}^*(\langle \mathscr{A}, L \rangle)$ is marked as "U", then we will say that $\mathscr{T}^*(\langle \mathscr{A}, h \rangle)$ *warrants* L and that L is *warranted* from Π_{AM}. (Warranted arguments correspond to those in the grounded extension of a Dung argumentation system [4].) There is a further requirement when the arguments in the dialectical tree contain presumptions—the conjunction of all presumptions used in even levels of the tree must be consistent. This can give rise to multiple trees for a given literal, as there can potentially be different arguments that make contradictory assumptions.

We can then extend the idea of a dialectical tree to a *dialectical forest*. For a given literal L, a dialectical forest $\mathscr{F}(L)$ consists of the set of dialectical trees for all arguments for L. We shall denote a marked dialectical forest, the set of all marked dialectical trees for arguments for L, as $\mathscr{F}^*(L)$. Hence, for a literal L, we say it is *warranted* if there is at least one argument for that literal in the dialectical forest $\mathscr{F}^*(L)$ that is labeled as "U", *not warranted* if there is at least one argument for the literal $\neg L$ in the dialectical forest $\mathscr{F}^*(\neg L)$ that is labeled as "U", and *undecided* otherwise.

With this, we have a complete description of the analytical model, and can go on to describe the DeLP3E framework.

3.3 The DeLP3E Framework

DeLP3E arises from the combination of the environmental model Π_{EM}, and the analytical model Π_{AM}; the two models are held together by the annotation function. This allows elements from the AM to be annotated with elements from the EM. These annotations specify the conditions under which the various statements in the AM can potentially be true.

Intuitively, given Π_{AM}, every element of $\Omega \cup \Theta \cup \Delta \cup \Phi$ might only hold in certain worlds in the set $\mathscr{W}_{EM}$—that is, they are subject to probabilistic events. Therefore, we associate elements of $\Omega \cup \Theta \cup \Delta \cup \Phi$ with a formula from *form*$_{EM}$.

---

[2]In the sense of providing reasons for and against a position.

$$\begin{array}{ll}
af(\theta_{1a}) = af(\theta_{1b}) = k \vee \left(f \wedge \left(h \vee (e \wedge l)\right)\right) & af(\phi_3) \qquad\qquad = b \\
af(\theta_2) \qquad\qquad = i & af(\delta_{1a}) = af(\delta_{1b}) = \text{True} \\
af(\omega_{1a}) = af(\omega_{1b}) = \text{True} & af(\delta_2) \qquad\qquad = \text{True} \\
af(\omega_{2a}) = af(\omega_{2b}) = \text{True} & af(\delta_3) \qquad\qquad = \text{True} \\
af(\phi_1) \qquad\qquad = c \vee a & af(\delta_4) \qquad\qquad = \text{True} \\
af(\phi_2) \qquad\qquad = f \wedge m & af(\delta_{5a}) = af(\delta_{5b}) = \text{True}
\end{array}$$

Fig. 3.3 Example annotation function

In doing so, we can in turn compute the probabilities of subsets of $\Omega \cup \Theta \cup \Delta \cup \Phi$ using the information contained in Π_{EM}, as we describe shortly. The notion of an *annotation function* associates elements of $\Omega \cup \Theta \cup \Delta \cup \Phi$ with elements of *form*$_{EM}$.

Definition 3.9 An *annotation function* is any function $af : \Omega \cup \Theta \cup \Delta \cup \Phi \rightarrow$ *form*$_{EM}$. We use $[af]$ to denote the set of all annotation functions.

Figure 3.3 shows an example of an annotation function.

   We will sometimes denote annotation functions as sets of pairs $(f, af(f))$ in order to simplify the presentation. Function *af* may come from an expert's knowledge or the data itself. Choosing the correct function and learning the function from data is the topic of ongoing work.

   We also note that, by using the annotation function, we may have certain statements that appear as both facts and presumptions (likewise for strict and defeasible rules). However, these constructs would have different annotations, and thus be applicable in different worlds. We note that the annotation function can allow AM facts and strict rules to be true in some EM worlds and false in others—this is why we include facts and strict rules as part of an argument in our framework.

Example 3.7 Suppose we added the following presumptions to the program in our running example:

$$\phi_3 = l \prec$$

$$\phi_4 = m \prec$$

and suppose we extend *af* as follows:

$$af(\phi_3) = a \wedge b$$

$$af(\phi_4) = a \wedge b \wedge c$$

So, for instance, unlike θ_1, ϕ_3 can potentially be true in any world of the form:

$$\{a, b\}$$

$\blacksquare$

We now have all the components to formally define DeLP3E programs.

Definition 3.10 Given environmental model Π_{EM}, analytical model Π_{AM}, and annotation function af, a DeLP3E *program* is of the form $\mathscr{I} = (\Pi_{EM}, \Pi_{AM}, af)$. We use notation $[\mathscr{I}]$ to denote the set of all possible programs.

The next step in the definition of DeLP3E is to explore entailment operations. In an entailment query, we are given an AM literal L, probability interval $p \pm \epsilon$, and DeLP3E program $\mathscr{I}$, and we wish to determine if L is entailed by $\mathscr{I}$ with a probability $p \pm \epsilon$. However, before we can formally define this entailment problem, we define a *warranting scenario* to determine the proper environment in question and the entailment bounds (Sect. 3.3.1). This is followed by our formal definition and method for computing entailment in Sect. 3.3.2.

3.3.1 Warranting Scenarios

In DeLP3E, we can consider a world-based approach; that is, the defeat relationship among arguments depends on the current state of the (EM) world.

Definition 3.11 Let $\mathscr{I} = (\Pi_{EM}, \Pi_{AM}, af)$ be a DeLP3E program, argument $\langle \mathscr{A}, L \rangle$ is *valid* w.r.t. world $w \in \mathscr{W}_{EM}$ iff $\forall c \in \mathscr{A}, w \models af(c)$.

We extend the notion of validity to argumentation lines, dialectical trees, and dialectical forests in the expected way (for instance, an argumentation line is valid w.r.t. w iff all arguments that comprise that line are valid w.r.t. w).

Example 3.8 Consider worlds $w_1, \ldots, w_8$ from Example 3.3 along with the argument $\langle \mathscr{A}_5, u \rangle$ from Example 3.4. This argument is valid in worlds w_1, w_2, w_3, w_4, w_6, and w_7. ∎

We also extend the idea of a dialectical tree w.r.t. worlds; so, for a given world $w \in \mathscr{W}_{EM}$, the dialectical (resp., marked dialectical) tree induced by w is denoted with $\mathscr{T}_w \langle \mathscr{A}, L \rangle$ (resp., $\mathscr{T}_w^* \langle \mathscr{A}, L \rangle$). We require that all arguments and defeaters in these trees be valid with respect to w. Likewise, we extend the notion of dialectical forests in the same manner (denoted with $\mathscr{F}_w(L)$ and $\mathscr{F}_w^*(L)$, resp.). Based on these concepts, we introduce the notion of *warranting scenario*.

Definition 3.12 Let $\mathscr{I} = (\Pi_{EM}, \Pi_{AM}, af)$ be a DeLP3E program and L be a literal formed with a ground atom from $\mathbf{G}_{AM}$; a world $w \in \mathscr{W}_{EM}$ is said to be a *warranting scenario* for L (denoted $w \vdash_{war} L$) iff there is a dialectical forest $\mathscr{F}_w^*(L)$ in which L is warranted and $\mathscr{F}_w^*(L)$ is valid w.r.t. w.

Note that a world w not being a warranting scenario for L, is not the same as it being a warranting scenario for $\neg L$. For that to be the case, we would need a dialectical tree $\mathscr{F}_w^*(\neg L)$ in which $\neg L$ is warranted and $\mathscr{F}_w^*(\neg L)$ is valid w.r.t. w.

Example 3.9 Considering the arguments from Example 3.8, worlds w_3, w_6, and w_7 are warranting scenarios for argument $\langle \mathscr{A}_5, u \rangle$. ∎

3.3.2 Entailment in DeLP3E

In this section, we use the idea of a warranting scenario to formally define our entailment problem. We first notice that the set of worlds in the EM where a literal L in the AM *must* be true is exactly the set of warranting scenarios—these are the "necessary" worlds:

$$nec(L) = \{w \in \mathscr{W}_{EM} \mid (w \vdash_{\text{war}} L)\}.$$

Now, the set of worlds in the EM where AM literal L *can* be true is the following—these are the "possible" worlds:

$$poss(L) = \{w \in \mathscr{W}_{EM} \mid w \nvdash_{\text{war}} \neg L\}.$$

Example 3.10 Following from Example 3.8, we have that:

$$nec(u) = \{w_3, w_6, w_7\} \text{ and } poss(u) = \{w_1, w_2, w_3, w_4, w_6, w_7\}.$$

∎

Definition 3.13 We define $for(w) = \bigwedge_{a \in w} a \wedge \bigwedge_{a \notin w} \neg a$, which denotes the *formula* that has w as its only model. Also, we extend this notation to sets of words: $for(W) = \bigvee_{w \in W} for(w)$.

Definition 3.14 (Entailment) Given DeLP3E program, $\mathscr{I} = (\Pi_{EM}, \Pi_{AM}, af)$, AM literal L and probability interval $p \pm \epsilon$, we say that $\mathscr{I}$ entails L with probability $p \pm \epsilon$ iff all probability distributions Pr that satisfy Π_{EM} satisfy $for(nec(L)) : p \pm \epsilon$ and $for(poss(L)) : p \pm \epsilon$.

We will also refer to the tightest bound $[p - \epsilon, p + \epsilon]$ such that $\mathscr{I}$ entails L with a probability $p \pm \epsilon$ as the "tightest entailment bounds." The intuition behind the above definition of entailment is as follows. Let ℓ be the maximum value for $p - \epsilon$ and u be the minimum value for $p + \epsilon$ before we can no longer say that $\mathscr{I}$ entails L with probability $p \pm \epsilon$. In this case, we can define probability distributions $Pr_{poss}^{-}, Pr_{poss}^{+}, Pr_{nec}^{-}, Pr_{nec}^{+}$ as follows:

- Pr_{poss}^{-} satisfies Π_{EM} and assigns the smallest possible probability to worlds that satisfy $for(poss(L))$.
- Pr_{poss}^{+} satisfies Π_{EM} and assigns the largest possible probability to worlds that satisfy $for(poss(L))$.
- Pr_{nec}^{-} satisfies Π_{EM} and assigns the smallest possible probability to worlds that satisfy $for(nec(L))$.
- Pr_{nec}^{+} satisfies Π_{EM} and assigns the largest possible probability to worlds that satisfy $for(nec(L))$.

We only need to compare $Pr_{poss}^{-}(poss(L))$ and $Pr_{nec}^{-}(nec(L))$ for finding the lower bound since $Pr_{poss}^{+}(poss(L)) \geq Pr_{poss}^{-}(poss(L))$ and $Pr_{nec}^{+}(nec(L)) \geq Pr_{nec}^{-}(nec(L))$.

Similar reasoning holds for the case of finding the upper bound. Thus, we get the following relationships:

$$\ell = \min \left(Pr^-_{poss}(poss(L)), Pr^-_{nec}(nec(L)) \right) \tag{3.1}$$

$$u = \max \left(Pr^+_{poss}(poss(L)), Pr^+_{nec}(nec(L)) \right) \tag{3.2}$$

However, we note that as $nec(L) \subseteq poss(L)$ we have the following:

$$\ell = Pr^-_{nec}\big(nec(L)\big) \tag{3.3}$$

$$u = Pr^+_{poss}\big(poss(L)\big) \tag{3.4}$$

Note that the values defined in Eqs. (3.3) and (3.4) are equivalent to the belief and plausibility values defined in Dempster-Shafer theory [18].

Hence, the tightest possible entailment bounds that can be assigned to a literal can be no less than the lower bound of the probability assigned to the necessary warranting scenarios and no more than the probability assigned to the possible warranting scenarios. Hence, we can compute the tightest probability bound such that L is entailed (denoted $\mathbf{P}_{L,Pr,\mathscr{I}}$) as follows:

$$\ell_{L,Pr,\mathscr{I}} = \sum_{w \in nec(L)} Pr^-_{nec(w)}, \quad u_{L,Pr,\mathscr{I}} = \sum_{w \in poss(L)} Pr^+_{poss(w)}$$

$$\ell_{L,Pr,\mathscr{I}} \leq \mathbf{P}_{L,Pr,\mathscr{I}} \leq u_{L,Pr,\mathscr{I}}$$

Thus, in interval form we have:

$$\mathbf{P}_{L,Pr,\mathscr{I}} = \left(\ell_{L,Pr,\mathscr{I}} + \frac{u_{L,Pr,\mathscr{I}} - \ell_{L,Pr,\mathscr{I}}}{2} \right) \pm \frac{u_{L,Pr,\mathscr{I}} - \ell_{L,Pr,\mathscr{I}}}{2}.$$

Now let us consider the computation of tightest probability bounds for entailment on a literal when we are given a knowledge base $\mathscr{K}_{EM}$ in the environmental model, which is specified in $\mathscr{I}$, instead of a probability distribution over all worlds. For a given world $w \in \mathscr{W}_{EM}$, let $for(w) = \left(\bigwedge_{a \in w} a \right) \wedge \left(\bigwedge_{a \notin w} \neg a \right)$—that is, a formula that is satisfied only by world w. Now we can determine the upper and lower bounds on the probability of a literal w.r.t. $\mathscr{K}_{EM}$ (denoted $\mathbf{P}_{L,\mathscr{I}}$) as follows:

$$\ell_{L,\mathscr{I}} = \text{EP-LP-MIN}\left(\mathscr{K}_{EM}, \bigvee_{w \in nec(L)} for(w) \right)$$

$$u_{L,\mathscr{I}} = \text{EP-LP-MAX} \left(\mathscr{K}_{EM}, \bigvee_{w \in poss(L)} for(w) \right)$$

$$\ell_{L,\mathscr{I}} \leq \mathbf{P}_{L,\mathscr{I}} \leq u_{L,\mathscr{I}}$$

Hence, $\mathbf{P}_{L,\mathscr{I}} = \left(\ell_{L,\mathscr{K}_{EM}} + \frac{u_{L,\mathscr{I}} - \ell_{L,\mathscr{I}}}{2} \right) \pm \frac{u_{L,\mathscr{I}} - \ell_{L,\mathscr{I}}}{2}$.

Example 3.11 Consider argument $\langle \mathscr{A}_5, u \rangle$ from Example 3.8. We can compute $\mathbf{P}_{u,\mathscr{I}}$ (where $\mathscr{I} = (\Pi'_{EM}, \Pi_{AM}, af)$).

Note that for the upper bound, the linear program we need to set up is the one shown in Example 3.3. For the lower bound, the objective function changes to: $\min x_3 + x_6 + x_7$. From these linear constraints, we obtain $\mathbf{P}_u = 0.7 \pm 0.2$.   ∎

In the following, we study the problem of consistency in our framework, which is the basis of the belief revision operators studied in the next chapter.

3.4   Consistency and Inconsistency in DeLP3E Programs

Even though our framework relies heavily on argumentation and reasoning under uncertainty, inconsistency in our knowledge base can still arise. For instance, the knowledge encoded in the environmental model could become contradictory, which would preclude any probability distribution from satisfying that part of the knowledge base. Even on the argumentation side, despite that fact that argumentation formalisms in general are inconsistency tolerant, there may be problems with inconsistency. For example, it would be problematic for DeLP3E if the set of strict facts and strict rules were contradictory, *and* the set of contradictory elements all arise under the same environmental conditions.

In this section, we explore what forms of inconsistency can arise in DeLP3E programs; this will form the basis for the material on belief revision, which is the topic of Chap. 4. We use the following notion of (classical) consistency of PreDeLP programs: Π is said to be *consistent* if there does not exist a ground literal a s.t. $\Pi \vdash a$ and $\Pi \vdash \neg a$. For DeLP3E programs, there are two main kinds of inconsistency that can be present; the first is what we refer to as EM, or Type I, (in)consistency.

Definition 3.15 An environmental model Π_{EM} is *Type I consistent* iff there exists a probability distribution Pr over the set of worlds $\mathscr{W}_{EM}$ that satisfies Π_{EM}.

We illustrate this type of consistency in the following example.

Example 3.12 It is possible to create probabilistic knowledge bases for which there is no satisfying probability distribution. The following formula is a simple example of such a case:

$$rain \vee hail : 0.4 \pm 0;$$

$$rain \wedge hail : 0.4 \pm 0.2.$$

The above is an example of Type I inconsistency in DeLP3E, as it arises from the fact that there is no satisfying interpretation for the EM knowledge base. ∎

However, even if the EM is consistent, the interaction between the annotation function and facts and strict rules can still cause another type of inconsistency to arise. We will refer to this as combined, or Type II, (in)consistency.

Definition 3.16 A DeLP3E program $\mathscr{I} = (\Pi_{EM}, \Pi_{AM}, af)$, with $\Pi_{AM} = \langle \Theta, \Omega, \Phi, \Delta \rangle$, is *Type II consistent* iff: given any probability distribution Pr that satisfies Π_{EM}, if there exists a world $w \in \mathscr{W}_{EM}$ such that $\bigcup_{x \in \Theta \cup \Omega \mid w \models af(x)} \{x\}$ is inconsistent, then we have $Pr(w) = 0$.

Thus, any EM world in which the set of associated facts and strict rules are inconsistent (we refer to this as "classical consistency") must always be assigned a zero probability. The intuition is as follows: any subset of facts and strict rules are thought to be true under certain circumstances—these circumstances are determined through the annotation function and can be expressed as sets of EM worlds. Suppose there is a world where two contradictory facts can both be considered to be true (based on the annotation function). If this occurs, then there must not exist a probability distribution that satisfies the program Π_{EM} that assigns such a world a non-zero probability, as this world leads to an inconsistency. We provide a more concrete example of Type II inconsistency next.

Example 3.13 Consider the environmental model from Example 3.2 (Page 22), the analytical model shown in Fig. 3.1 (Page 26), and the annotation function shown in Fig. 3.3 (Page 30). Suppose the following fact is added to the argumentation model:

$$\theta_3 = \neg p,$$

and that the annotation function is expanded as follows:

$$af(\theta_3) = k \wedge \neg f$$

Clearly, fact θ_3 is in direct conflict with fact θ_{1a}. However, this does not necessarily mean that there is an inconsistency. For instance, by the annotation function, θ_{1a} holds in the world $\{k, f\}$ while θ_3 does not. However, let's consider following world $w = \{k\}$. Note that $w \models af(\theta_3)$ and $w \models af(\theta_2)$. Hence, in this world both contradictory facts can occur. However, can this world be assigned a non-zero probability? A simple examination of the environmental model indicates that it can. Hence, in this case, we have Type II inconsistency. ∎

We say that a DeLP3E program is *consistent* iff it is both Type I and Type II consistent. However, in this chapter, we focus on Type II consistency and assume that the program is Type I consistent.

Algorithm CON-CHK-BFS($\Pi_{EM}, \Pi_{AM}, af, d, \mathscr{S} = \{S_1, \ldots, S_n\}$)

1. $\mathscr{S}' := \emptyset$
2. For each $S_i \in \mathscr{S}$ where S_i is not classically consistent, do the following:
    a. If Pr is such that $Pr \models \Pi_{EM}$ and $Pr(\bigwedge_{s \in S_i} af(s)) > 0$ then
        return INCONSISTENT and terminate;
    b. Else, $\mathscr{S}' := \mathscr{S}' \cup \{S' \subseteq S_i \mid |S'| = |S_i| - 1\}$;
3. If $d = 1$ return CONSISTENT;
4. Else, return CON-CHK-BFS($\Pi_{EM}, \Pi_{AM}, af, d - 1, \mathscr{S}'$).

Fig. 3.4 A straightforward BFS-based algorithm for consistency checking

Figure 3.4 gives a straightforward approach to identifying Type II inconsistent DeLP3E programs by running breath-first search on a set of $\Theta \cup \Omega$. The algorithm works by examining all subsets of a set of facts and strict rules to find inconsistent subsets whose corresponding formula in the environmental model can be assigned a non-zero probability. The following result states its correctness.

Proposition 3.1 *For Type I consistent DeLP3E program* $\mathscr{I} = (\Pi_{EM}, \Pi_{AM}, af)$ *where* Θ *and* Ω *are the sets of facts and strict rules in* Π_{AM}, *then* CON-CHK-BFS($\Pi_{EM}, \Pi_{AM}, af, d, \{\Theta \cup \Omega\}$) *(where* $d = |\Theta \cup \Omega|$) *returns* INCONSISTENT *iff the DeLP3E is Type II inconsistent.*

However, we note that even with an oracle for checking the classical consistency of a subset (line 2) and for determining the upper bound on the probability of the annotations (line 2a), this algorithm is still intractable as it explores all subsets of $\Theta \cup \Omega$. One possible way to attack this intractability is to restrict the depth of the search by setting d to be less than the size of $\Theta \cup \Omega$. In this case, we get the following result:

Proposition 3.2 *Given Type I consistent DeLP3E program* $\mathscr{I} = (\Pi_{EM}, \Pi_{AM}, af)$, *where* Θ *and* Ω *are the sets of facts and strict rules in* Π_{AM} *and* $d < |\Theta \cup \Omega|$, *then if* CON-CHK-BFS($\Pi_{EM}, \Pi_{AM}, af, d, \{\Theta \cup \Omega\}$) *returns* INCONSISTENT, *the program* $\mathscr{I}$ *is Type II inconsistent.*

Therefore, by restricting depth, we can view this algorithm as an "anytime" approach, essentially searching for a world leading to an inconsistent program and not halting until it does.

In the next chapter, we will explore three main methods for resolving Type II inconsistencies by applying belief revision operators.

3.5 Case Study: An Application in Cybersecurity

In this section we develop a complete example of how the DeLP3E framework can be used to deal with a cyber attribution problem. In this scenario, a cyberattack has been detected and we want to determine who is responsible for it.

3.5.1 Model for the Attribution Problem

To specify the model we need to specify the environmental model, the analytical model, and the annotation function. First we identify two special subsets of the set of constants (**C**) for this application: $\mathbf{C}_{act}$ and $\mathbf{C}_{ops}$, which specify the actors that could conduct cyberoperations and the operations themselves, respectively:

$$\mathbf{C}_{act} = \{baja, krasnovia, mojave\}$$

$$\mathbf{C}_{ops} = \{worm123\}$$

That is, the possible actors are the states of *baja*, *krasnovia* and *mojave*, and the only operation that we consider they can conduct is a *worm123* attack.

Next, we need to specify the sets of predicates, $\mathbf{P}_{EM}$, the predicates for the environmental model, and $\mathbf{P}_{AM}$, the predicates for the analytical model. These are given in Fig. 3.5, which presents all the predicates with variables. The following are examples of ground atoms over those predicates; again, we distinguish between the subset of ground atoms from the environmental model $\mathbf{G}_{EM}$ and the ground atoms from the analytical model $\mathbf{G}_{AM}$:

$\mathbf{P}_{EM}$:	$origIP(M,X)$	Malware M originated from an IP address belonging to actor X.
	$malwInOp(M,O)$	Malware M was used in cyberoperation O.
	$mwHint(M,X)$	Malware M contained a hint that it was created by actor X.
	$compilLang(M,C)$	Malware M was compiled in a system that used language C.
	$nativLang(X,C)$	Language C is the native language of actor X.
	$inLgConf(X,X')$	Actors X,X' are in a larger conflict with each other.
	$mseTT(X,N)$	The number of top-tier math-science-engineering universities in country X is at least N.
	$infGovSys(X,M)$	Systems belonging to actor X were infected with malware M.
	$cybCapAge(X,N)$	Actor X has had a cyberwarfare capability for N years or less.
	$govCybLab(X)$	Actor X has a government cybersecurity lab.
$\mathbf{P}_{AM}$:	$condOp(X,O)$	Actor X conducted cyberoperation O.
	$evidOf(X,O)$	There is evidence that actor X conducted cyberoperation O.
	$motiv(X,X')$	Actor X had a motive to launch a cyberattack against actor X'.
	$isCap(X,O)$	Actor X is capable of conducting cyberoperation O.
	$tgt(X,O)$	Actor X was the target of cyberoperation O.
	$hasMseInvest(X)$	Actor X has a significant investment in math-science-engineering education.
	$expCw(X)$	Actor X has experience in conducting cyberoperations.

Fig. 3.5 Predicate definitions for the environment and analytical models in the cyber attribution example

G$_{EM}$: $origIP(mw123sam1, krasnovia), mwHint(mw123sam1, krasnovia),$

$inLgConf(krasnovia, baja), mseTT(krasnovia, 2)$

G$_{AM}$: $evidOf(mojave, worm123), motiv(baja, krasnovia), expCw(baja),$

$tgt(krasnovia, worm123)$

P$_{AM}$ and the set of constants provides all the information we need for the analytical model. However, there is more to the environmental model than just **P**$_{EM}$ and the constants. We need to specify the probabilities of formulas. This information is given by the following set of probabilistic formulas $\mathscr{K}_{EM}$:

$f_1 = govCybLab(baja) : 0.7 \pm 0.2$

$f_2 = cybCapAge(baja, 5) : 0.3 \pm 0.1$

$f_3 = mseTT(baja, 2) : 0.8 \pm 0.2$

$f_4 = mwHint(mw123sam1, mojave) \wedge compilLang(worm123, english) : 0.8 \pm 0.1$

$f_5 = malwInOp(mw123sam1, worm123)$

$\wedge\ malwareRel(mw123sam1, mw123sam2)$

$\wedge\ mwHint(mw123sam2, mojave) : 0.5 \pm 0.2$

$f_6 = inLgConf(baja, krasnovia) \vee \neg cooper(baja, krasnovia) : 0.9 \pm 0.1$

$f_7 = origIP(mw123sam1, baja) : 1 \pm 0$

Given this probabilistic information, we can demonstrate the linear programming approach to the *maximum entailment* problem defined in Definition 3.2. Consider knowledge base $\mathscr{K}'_{EM}$ and a set of ground atoms restricted to those that appear in that program. Hence, we have the following worlds:

$w_1 = \{govCybLab(baja), cybCapAge(baja, 5), mseTT(baja, 2)\}$

$w_2 = \{govCybLab(baja), cybCapAge(baja, 5)\}$

$w_3 = \{govCybLab(baja), mseTT(baja, 2)\}$

$w_4 = \{cybCapAge(baja, 5), mseTT(baja, 2)\}$

$w_5 = \{cybCapAge(baja, 5)\}$

$w_6 = \{govCybLab(baja)\}$

$w_7 = \{mseTT(baja, 2)\}$

$w_8 = \emptyset$

and suppose we wish to compute the probability for formula:

$$q = govCybLab(baja) \lor mseTT(baja, 2)$$

For each formula in $\mathscr{K}_{EM}$ we have a constraint, and for each world above we have a variable. An objective function is created based on the worlds that satisfy the query formula (in this case, worlds $w_1, w_2, w_3, w_4, w_6, w_7$). Hence, EP-LP-MIN($\mathscr{K}'_{EM}, q$) can be written as follows:

$$
\begin{array}{rcl}
\max & x_1 + x_2 + x_3 + x_4 + x_6 + x_7 & w.r.t. : \\
0.6 \leq & x_1 + x_2 + x_3 + x_6 & \leq 0.8 \\
0.2 \leq & x_1 + x_2 + x_4 + x_5 & \leq 0.4 \\
0.8 \leq & x_1 + x_3 + x_4 + x_7 & \leq 1 \\
& x_1 + x_2 + x_3 + x_4 + x_5 + x_6 + x_7 + x_8 = 1 &
\end{array}
$$

From this, we can solve EP-LP-MAX($\mathscr{K}'_{EM}, q$) and, after an easy modification, EP-LP-MIN($\mathscr{K}'_{EM}, q$), and obtain the solution 0.9 ± 0.1.

Now, given $\mathbf{P}_{AM}$ and $\mathbf{C}$, we can assemble the ground argumentation framework of Fig. 3.6 as a sample Π_{AM}. From this argumentation framework, we can build the following arguments:

$$
\begin{array}{ll}
\langle \mathscr{A}_1, condOp(baja, worm123) \rangle & \mathscr{A}_1 = \{\theta_{1a}, \delta_{1a}\} \\
\langle \mathscr{A}_2, condOp(baja, worm123) \rangle & \mathscr{A}_2 = \{\phi_1, \phi_2, \delta_4, \omega_{2a}, \theta_{1a}, \theta_2\} \\
\langle \mathscr{A}_3, condOp(baja, worm123) \rangle & \mathscr{A}_3 = \{\phi_1, \delta_2, \delta_4\} \\
\langle \mathscr{A}_4, condOp(baja, worm123) \rangle & \mathscr{A}_4 = \{\phi_2, \delta_3, \theta_2\} \\
\langle \mathscr{A}_5, isCap(baja, worm123) \rangle & \mathscr{A}_5 = \{\phi_1, \delta_4\} \\
\langle \mathscr{A}_6, \neg condOp(baja, worm123) \rangle & \mathscr{A}_6 = \{\delta_{1b}, \theta_{1b}, \omega_{1a}\} \\
\langle \mathscr{A}_7, \neg isCap(baja, worm123) \rangle & \mathscr{A}_7 = \{\phi_3, \delta_{5a}\}
\end{array}
$$

Note that:

$$\langle \mathscr{A}_5, isCap(baja, worm123) \rangle$$

is a sub-argument of both

$$\langle \mathscr{A}_2, condOp(baja, worm123) \rangle$$

and

$$\langle \mathscr{A}_3, condOp(baja, worm123) \rangle$$

Θ : $\theta_{1a} = evidOf(baja, worm123)$
  $\theta_{1b} = evidOf(mojave, worm123)$
  $\theta_2 = motiv(baja, krasnovia)$

Ω : $\omega_{1a} = \neg condOp(baja, worm123) \leftarrow condOp(mojave, worm123)$
  $\omega_{1b} = \neg condOp(mojave, worm123) \leftarrow condOp(baja, worm123)$
  $\omega_{2a} = condOp(baja, worm123) \leftarrow$
      $evidOf(baja, worm123),$
      $isCap(baja, worm123),$
      $motiv(baja, krasnovia),$
      $tgt(krasnovia, worm123)$
  $\omega_{2b} = condOp(mojave, worm123) \leftarrow$
      $evidOf(mojave, worm123),$
      $isCap(mojave, worm123),$
      $motiv(mojave, krasnovia),$
      $tgt(krasnovia, worm123)$

Φ : $\phi_1 = hasMseInvest(baja) \prec$
  $\phi_2 = tgt(krasnovia, worm123) \prec$
  $\phi_3 = \neg expCw(baja) \prec$

Δ : $\delta_{1a} = condOp(baja, worm123) \prec evidOf(baja, worm123)$
  $\delta_{1b} = condOp(mojave, worm123) \prec evidOf(mojave, worm123)$
  $\delta_2 = condOp(baja, worm123) \prec isCap(baja, worm123)$
  $\delta_3 = condOp(baja, worm123) \prec$
      $motiv(baja, krasnovia),$
      $tgt(krasnovia, worm123)$
  $\delta_4 = isCap(baja, worm123) \prec hasMseInvest(baja)$
  $\delta_{5a} = \neg isCap(baja, worm123) \prec \neg expCw(baja)$
  $\delta_{5b} = \neg isCap(mojave, worm123) \prec \neg expCw(mojave)$

Fig. 3.6 A ground argumentation framework

The following are some of the attack relationships between these arguments: $\mathscr{A}_1$, $\mathscr{A}_2$, $\mathscr{A}_3$, and $\mathscr{A}_4$ all attack $\mathscr{A}_6$; $\mathscr{A}_5$ attacks $\mathscr{A}_7$; and $\mathscr{A}_7$ attacks $\mathscr{A}_2$.

In Fig. 3.7 we show an another example of a knowledge base for the attribution problem, this time with a non-ground argumentation system.

With the environmental and analytical models specified, the remaining component of the model is the annotation function; one suitable annotation function is given in Fig. 3.8. Consider worlds $w_1, \ldots, w_8$ along with the argument $\langle \mathscr{A}_5, isCap(baja, worm123) \rangle$. This argument is valid in worlds w_1, w_2, w_3, w_4, w_6, and w_7. Similarly, worlds w_3, w_6, and w_7 are warranting scenarios for argument $\langle \mathscr{A}_5, isCap(baja, worm123) \rangle$ and

$$nec(isCap(baja, worm123)) = \{w_3, w_6, w_7\}$$

while

$$poss(isCap(baja, worm123)) = \{w_1, w_2, w_3, w_4, w_6, w_7\}$$

$$
\begin{aligned}
\Theta : \; \theta_1 &= evidOf(baja, worm123) \\
\theta_2 &= motiv(baja, krasnovia)
\end{aligned}
$$

$$
\begin{aligned}
\Omega : \; \omega_1 &= \neg condOp(X, O) \leftarrow condOp(X', O), X \neq X' \\
\omega_2 &= condOp(X, O) \leftarrow evidOf(X, O), isCap(X, O), \\
&\quad motiv(X, X'), tgt(X', O), X \neq X'
\end{aligned}
$$

$$
\begin{aligned}
\Phi : \; \phi_1 &= hasMseInvest(baja) \prec \\
\phi_2 &= tgt(krasnovia, worm123) \prec \\
\phi_3 &= \neg expCw(baja) \prec
\end{aligned}
$$

$$
\begin{aligned}
\Delta : \; \delta_1 &= condOp(X, O) \prec evidOf(X, O) \\
\delta_2 &= condOp(X, O) \prec isCap(X, O) \\
\delta_3 &= condOp(X, O) \prec motiv(X, X'), tgt(X', O) \\
\delta_4 &= isCap(X, O) \prec hasMseInvest(X) \\
\delta_5 &= \neg isCap(X, O) \prec \neg expCw(X)
\end{aligned}
$$

Fig. 3.7 A non-ground argumentation framework

$$
\begin{aligned}
af(\theta_1) &= origIP(worm123, baja) \vee \big(malwInOp(worm123, o) \wedge \\
&\quad \big(mwHint(worm123, baja) \vee (compilLang(worm123, c) \wedge nativLang(baja, c))\big)\big) \\
af(\theta_2) &= inLgConf(baja, krasnovia) \\
af(\omega_1) &= \mathsf{True} \\
af(\omega_2) &= \mathsf{True} \\
af(\phi_1) &= mseTT(baja, 2) \vee govCybLab(baja) \\
af(\phi_2) &= malwInOp(worm123, o') \wedge infGovSys(krasnovia, worm123) \\
af(\phi_3) &= cybCapAge(baja, 5) \\
af(\delta_1) &= \mathsf{True} \\
af(\delta_2) &= \mathsf{True} \\
af(\delta_3) &= \mathsf{True} \\
af(\delta_4) &= \mathsf{True} \\
af(\delta_5) &= \mathsf{True}
\end{aligned}
$$

Fig. 3.8 Example annotation function

3.5.2 Applying Entailment to the Cyber Attribution Problem

We now discuss how finding tight bounds on the entailment probability can be applied to the cyber attribution problem. Following the domain-specific notation introduced in the beginning of this case study (where the set of constants $\mathbf{C}$ includes two subsets: $\mathbf{C}_{act}$ and $\mathbf{C}_{ops}$, that specify the actors that could conduct cyberoperations and the operations themselves, respectively), we define a special case of the entailment problem as follows.

Definition 3.17 Let $\mathscr{I} = (\Pi_{EM}, \Pi_{AM}, af)$ be a DeLP3E program, $\mathscr{S} \subseteq \mathbf{C}_{act}$ (the set of "suspects"), $\mathscr{O} \in \mathbf{C}_{ops}$ (the "operation"), $e \subseteq \mathbf{G}_{EM}$ (the "evidence"), and $\mathscr{D} \subseteq \mathbf{G}_{EM}$ (the "probabilistic fact").

Algorithm SFWD_ATTRIB(i, $\mathscr{S}$, $\mathscr{O}$, e)

1. Let $\mathscr{I}' = (\Pi_{EM}, \Pi_{AM} \cup e, af')$, where $af'(c) = \top$ if $c \in e$
       and $af'(c) = af(c)$ otherwise.
2. For each $A \in \mathscr{S}$ and $w \in \mathscr{W}_{EM}$ do
3. $Pos := \mathscr{F}_w^*(condOp(A, \mathscr{O}))$ w.r.t. $\mathscr{I}'$;
4. $Neg := \mathscr{F}_w^*(\neg condOp(A, \mathscr{O}))$ w.r.t. $\mathscr{I}'$;
5. For each $A \in \mathscr{S}$ do
6. $m := nec(condOp(A, \mathscr{O}))$ w.r.t. Π_{EM} and af' (computed using Pos);
7. $c := poss(condOp(A, \mathscr{O}))$ w.r.t. Π_{EM} and af' (computed using Neg);
8. $P_A := \mathbf{P}_{condOp(A, \mathscr{O}), \mathscr{I}'}$;
9. Return $\arg\max_A (P_A)$.

Fig. 3.9 A straightforward algorithm for finding a solution to an attribution query

An actor $A \in \mathscr{S}$ is said to be a *most probable suspect* iff there does not exist $A' \in \mathscr{S}$ such that the midpoint of $\mathbf{P}_{condOp(A', \mathscr{O}), \mathscr{I}'}$ is greater than the midpoint of $\mathbf{P}_{condOp(A, \mathscr{O}), \mathscr{I}'}$, where $\mathscr{I}' = (\Pi_{EM} \cup \Pi_e \cup \Pi_{\mathscr{D}}, \Pi_{AM}, af')$ with $\Pi_e = \bigcup_{c \in e}\{c : 1 \pm 0\}$ and $\Pi_{\mathscr{D}} = \bigcup_{c \in \mathscr{D}}\{c : p \pm \epsilon\}$.

Note that we use midpoints of $\mathbf{P}_{condOp(A', \mathscr{O}), \mathscr{I}'}$ and $\mathbf{P}_{condOp(A, \mathscr{O}), \mathscr{I}'}$ to compare intervals; alternative formulations are possible based on the upper or lower bounds of these intervals.

Given the above definition, we refer to $Q = (\mathscr{I}, \mathscr{S}, \mathscr{O}, e)$ as an *attribution query*, and A as an *answer* to Q. We note that in the above definition, the items of evidence are added to the environmental model with a probability of 1. While in general this may be the case, there are often instances in analysis of a cyberoperation where the evidence may be true with some degree of uncertainty; for this reason, we are allowing probabilistic facts in the definition.

To understand how uncertain evidence can be present in a cybersecurity setting, consider the following scenario:

> In Symantec's initial analysis of the Stuxnet worm, analysts found the routine designed to attack the S7-417 logic controller was incomplete, and hence would not function [5]. However, industrial control system expert Ralph Langner claimed that the incomplete code would run provided a missing data block is generated, which he thought was possible [11]. In this case, though the code was incomplete, uncertainty was clearly present regarding its usability.[3]

This situation provides a real-world example of the need to compare arguments—in this case, in the worlds where both arguments are valid, Langner's argument would likely defeat Symantec's by generalized specificity (the outcome, of course, will depend on the exact formalization of the two).

In Fig. 3.9 we give a simple, straightforward algorithm for attribution queries. The correctness of this algorithm clearly follows from the definitions above. We note

---

[3]Langner was later vindicated by the discovery of an older sample, Stuxnet 0.5, which generated the data block [3].

that a key source of computational complexity lies in step 2, where all arguments supporting the hypothesis that each actor conducted the operation are computed *for each world in the EM*; this leads to a factor of $2^{|\mathbf{G}_{EM}|}$ (exponential in the number of ground atoms in the environmental model). However, we also note that this is equal to the time complexity required to write out a linear program for answering the entailment query.

Note that the exact approaches presented thus far for answering attribution queries experience exponential running times in the worst case. Hence, for the creation of a real-world system, we consider several practical approaches that can be taken to answer attribution queries $Q = (i, \mathscr{S}, \mathscr{O}, e)$. We are currently exploring several of these ideas as we work to build a system for cyber attribution based on DeLP3E:

1. *Approximating the warranting formula:* Instead of inspecting all possible classical dialectical trees as in Approach 1, either a subset of trees can be computed according to a given heuristic or an anytime approach can be adopted to select such a subset $\mathscr{F}'$. The computations with respect to F' will then yield sound approximations relative to the full forest $\mathscr{F}$, which means that all probability intervals will be supersets of the exact intervals.
2. *Approximating the probability:* Another alternative to Approach 1 is to apply approximation algorithms to the formula; for instance:
   a. Approximate satisfiability: if the formula is unsatisfiable, then the warranting probability is zero;
   b. A lower bound on the warranting probability can be obtained from a subset of possible worlds (k most probable worlds, random sample of worlds, etc.).
3. *"What-if" Reasoning:* Given a set $\mathscr{W}_{int}$ of worlds of interest and a warranting formula ϕ (computed using any of the above approaches), each world can be checked to see which literals $condOp(A_i, \mathscr{O})$, with $A_i \in \mathscr{S}$, are warranted. That is, instead of computing probability of attribution, the attribution literal is analyzed in each world of interest.

3.6 Conclusions

In this chapter we introduced the DeLP3E framework, consisting of an environmental model, an analytical model, and an annotation function that relates the two [20]. DeLP3E is an extension of the PreDeLP language in which sentences can be annotated with probabilistic events. Such events are connected to a probabilistic model, allowing a clear separation of interests between certain and uncertain knowledge while allowing uncertainty to be captured and incorporated into reasoning. After presenting the language, we discussed the types of inconsistencies that can arise in DeLP3E programs, setting up the topic of belief revision, which is discussed in detail in the next chapter. Finally, we presented an extended case study of the application of DeLP3E to the attribution problem.

This model is of interest to both the argumentation literature, in showing how argumentation can be applied to a complex real-world problem, and to the cybersecurity literature, suggesting tools that can be used to address this problem. As part of the case study we considered a special kind of query, called an attribution query, that is useful in tackling the problem of attributing responsibility to entities given a cyberevent of interest.

References

1. C. E. Alchourrón, P. Gärdenfors, and D. Makinson. On the logic of theory change: Partial meet contraction and revision functions. *J. Sym. Log.*, 50(2):510–530, 1985.
2. C. Altheide. *Digital Forensics with Open Source Tools*. Syngress, 2011.
3. S. Corp. Stuxnet 0.5: Disrupting Uranium Processing at Natanz. *Symantec Connect*, Feb. 2013.
4. P. M. Dung. On the acceptability of arguments and its fundamental role in nonmonotonic reasoning, logic programming and *n*-person games. *Artificial Intelligence*, 77:pp. 321–357, 1995.
5. N. Falliere, L. O. Murchu, and E. Chien. W32.Stuxnet Dossier Version 1.4. *Symantec Corporation*, Feb. 2011.
6. A. J. García and G. R. Simari. Defeasible logic programming: An argumentative approach. *Theory and Practice of Logic Programming*, 4(1-2):95–138, 2004.
7. P. Gardenfors. *Knowledge in flux: modeling the dynamics of epistemic states*. MIT Press, Cambridge, Mass., 1988.
8. P. Gärdenfors. *Belief revision*, volume 29. Cambridge University Press, 2003.
9. R. J. Heuer. *Psychology of Intelligence Analysis*. Center for the Study of Intelligence, 1999.
10. S. Khuller, M. V. Martinez, D. S. Nau, A. Sliva, G. I. Simari, and V. S. Subrahmanian. Computing most probable worlds of action probabilistic logic programs: scalable estimation for $10^{30,000}$ worlds. *Annals of Mathematics and Artificial Intelligence*, 51(2-4):295–331, 2007.
11. R. Langner. Matching Langner Stuxnet analysis and Symantic dossier update. *Langner Communications GmbH*, Feb. 2011.
12. J. W. Lloyd. *Foundations of Logic Programming, 2nd Edition*. Springer, 1987.
13. M. V. Martinez, A. J. García, and G. R. Simari. On the use of presumptions in structured defeasible reasoning. In *Proceedings of the International Conference on Computational Models of Argument (COMMA)*, pages 185–196, 2012.
14. N. J. Nilsson. Probabilistic logic. *Artificial Intelligence*, 28(1):71–87, 1986.
15. I. Rahwan and G. R. Simari. *Argumentation in Artificial Intelligence*. Springer, 2009.
16. L. Riley, K. Atkinson, T. R. Payne, and E. Black. An implemented dialogue system for inquiry and persuasion. In *Proceedings of the International Workshop on Theory and Applications of Formal Argumentation (TAFA)*, pages 67–84. Springer, 2011.
17. Shadows in the Cloud: Investigating Cyber Espionage 2.0. Technical report, Information Warfare Monitor and Shadowserver Foundation, April 2010.
18. G. Shafer et al. *A mathematical theory of evidence*, volume 1. Princeton university press Princeton, 1976.
19. P. Shakarian, J. Shakarian, and A. Ruef. *Introduction to Cyber-Warfare: A Multidisciplinary Approach*. Syngress, 2013.
20. P. Shakarian, G. I. Simari, G. Moores, D. Paulo, S. Parsons, M. A. Falappa, and A. Aleali. Belief revision in structured probabilistic argumentation. *Annals of Mathematics and Artificial Intelligence*, 78(3-4):259–301, 2016.

21. G. R. Simari and R. P. Loui. A mathematical treatment of defeasible reasoning and its implementation. *Artificial Intelligence*, 53(2-3):125–157, 1992.
22. G. I. Simari, M. V. Martinez, A. Sliva, and V. S. Subrahmanian. Focused most probable world computations in probabilistic logic programs. *Annals of Mathematics and Artificial Intelligence*, 64(2-3):113–143, 2012.
23. L. Spitzner. Honeypots: Catching the Insider Threat. In *Proceedings of the Computer Security Applications Conference*, pages 170–179. IEEE Computer Society, 2003.
24. F. Stolzenburg, A. García, C. I. Chesñevar, and G. R. Simari. Computing Generalized Specificity. *Journal of Non-Classical Logics*, 13(1):87–113, 2003.
25. O. Thonnard, W. Mees, and M. Dacier. On a multicriteria clustering approach for attack attribution. *SIGKDD Explorations*, 12(1):11–20, 2010.

Chapter 4
Belief Revision in DeLP3E

4.1 Introduction

Many real-world knowledge-based systems must deal with information coming
from different sources that invariably leads to uncertain content, be it from gaps
in knowledge (incompleteness), over specification (inconsistency), or because the
knowledge is inherently uncertain (such as weather forecasts or measurements
that are necessarily imprecise). Far from considering such uncertain knowledge
useless, knowledge engineers face the challenge of putting it to its best possible
use when solving a wide range of problems. In particular, one basic problem
that needs to be investigated in depth is that of *revising* such knowledge bases
in a principled manner. In this chapter, we tackle the problem of carrying out
belief revision operations in the DeLP3E model introduced in Chap. 3. We begin
with the proposal of two sets of rationality postulates characterizing how such
operations should behave: one for the analytical model and one for the annotation
function (as we show, revising the environmental model is not sufficient to restore
consistency). These postulates are based on the classical approach proposed in [7]
for non-prioritized belief revision in classical knowledge bases. We then study two
classes of operators and their theoretical relationships with the proposed postulates,
concluding with representation theorems for each class. Then, we propose a subclass
of the annotation function-based operators called **QAFO** that takes *quantitative*
aspects into account when performing revisions, such as how the probabilities of
certain literals or formulas of interest change after the revision takes place.

4.2 Basic Belief Revision

We now explore three methods for resolving inconsistencies of Type II (cf.
Sect. 3.4); they can be briefly summarized as follows:

© The Author(s) 2018
E. Nunes et al., *Artificial Intelligence Tools for Cyber Attribution*, SpringerBriefs in
Computer Science, https://doi.org/10.1007/978-3-319-73788-1_4

Revise the EM.   The probabilistic model can be changed in order to force the
worlds that induce contradicting strict knowledge to have probability zero. In
general, this type of revision by itself is not ideal as it will not work in all cases.
We discuss this method in Sect. 4.2.1.

Revise the AM.   The argumentation model can be changed in such a way that
the set of strict rules and facts is consistent. If this is the case, then Type II
consistency follows. We discuss this method in Sect. 4.2.2.

Revise the annotation function.   The annotations involved in the inconsistency can
be changed so that the conflicting information in the AM does not become
induced under any possible world. This can be viewed as a generalization of
AM revision. We discuss this method in Sect. 4.2.3.

4.2.1   EM-Based Belief Revision

We now study belief revision through updating the environmental model only
(Π_{EM}). Suppose that Π_{EM} is consistent, but that the overall program is Type II
inconsistent. Then, there must exist a set of worlds in the EM such that there exists a
probability distribution that assigns each of them a non-zero probability. This gives
rise to the following result.

Proposition 4.1 *If there exists a probability distribution* Pr *that satisfies* Π_{EM}
s.t. there exists a world $w \in \mathcal{W}_{EM}$ *where* $Pr(w) > 0$ *and* $\bigcup_{x \in \Theta \cup \Omega \,|\, w \models af(x)} \{x\}$ *is*
inconsistent (Type II inconsistency), then any change made in order to resolve this
inconsistency by modifying only Π_{EM} *yields a new EM* Π'_{EM} *such that* $\left(\bigwedge_{a \in w} a \wedge \bigwedge_{a \notin w} \neg a \right) : 0 \pm 0$ *is entailed by* Π'_{EM}.

Proposition 4.1 seems to imply an easy strategy to resolve Type II inconsistencies: add formulas to Π_{EM} forcing the necessary worlds to have a zero probability.
However, this may lead to Type I inconsistencies in the resulting model Π'_{EM}. If we
are applying an EM-only strategy to resolve inconsistencies, this would then lead to
further adjustments to Π'_{EM} in order to restore Type I consistency. We illustrate this
situation in the following example.

Example 4.1 Consider two contradictory facts in an AM: a and $\neg a$ such that
$af(a) = p$ and $af(\neg a) = q$. Suppose that p and q are the only atoms in the EM, and
that we have:

$$p : 0.4 \pm 0$$
$$q : 0.8 \pm 0.1$$
$$\neg p \wedge \neg q : 0.2 \pm 0.1$$

which is consistent since the following distribution satisfies all constraints:

$Pr(\{p\}) = 0.2$;
$Pr(\{p, q\}) = 0.2$;
$Pr(\{q\}) = 0.5$;
$Pr(\{\}) = 0.1$.

Now, to restore Type II consistency of our simple DeLP3E program, we can add formula $p \wedge q : 0 \pm 0$ to the EM so that world $\{p, q\}$ is forced to have probability zero. However, this leads to another inconsistency, this time of Type I, since putting together all the constraints we have:

$Pr(\{p, q\}) = 0;$
$Pr(\{p\}) + Pr(\{p, q\}) = 0.4;$
$Pr(\{q\}) + Pr(\{p, q\}) = 0.8 \pm 0.1;$
$Pr(\{\}) = 0.2 \pm 0.1;$
$Pr(\{p\}) + Pr(\{p, q\}) + Pr(\{q\}) + Pr(\{\}) = 1;$

which is clearly inconsistent. Repairing this inconsistency involves changing the EM further, for instance by relaxing the bounds in the first two formulas to accommodate the probability mass that world $\{p, q\}$ had before and can no longer hold. ∎

In the previous example, we saw how changes made to repair Type II inconsistencies could lead to Type I inconsistencies. It is also possible that changing Π'_{EM} (for instance, by removing elements, relaxing probability bounds of the sentences, etc.) causes Type II inconsistency in the overall DeLP3E program—this would lead to the need to set more EM worlds to a probability of zero. Unfortunately, this process is not guaranteed to arrive at a fully consistent program before being unable to continue; consider the following example, where the process cannot even begin.

Example 4.2   Consider an AM composed of several contradictory facts, an EM with just two atoms (as in the previous example), and the following annotation function:

$af(a) = p \qquad af(b) = \neg p \qquad af(c) = \neg p \quad af(d) = q$
$af(\neg a) = q \quad af(\neg b) = \neg q \quad af(\neg c) = p \quad af(\neg d) = \neg q$

Modifying the EM so that no two contradictory literals ever hold at once in a world that has a non-zero probability leads to the constraints:

$Pr(\{p, q\}) = 0;$
$Pr(\{p\}) = 0;$
$Pr(\{q\}) = 0;$
$Pr(\{\}) = 0;$
$Pr(\{p\}) + Pr(\{p, q\}) + Pr(\{q\}) + Pr(\{\}) = 1;$

As in the previous example, the probability mass cannot be accommodated within these constraints. It would thus be impossible to restore consistency by only modifying Π_{EM}. ∎

We thus arrive at the following observation from Example 4.2:

Observation 1 *Given a Type II inconsistent DeLP3E program, consistency cannot always be restored via modifications to Π_{EM} alone.*

Therefore, due to this line of reasoning, in this chapter we focus our efforts on modifications to the other two components of a DeLP3E framework: the AM and the annotation function, as described in the next two sections. Approaches combining two or more of these methods are the topic of future work.

4.2.2 AM-Based Belief Revision

The result of the previous section indicates that EM-based belief revision of a
DeLP3E framework (at least by itself) is not a tenable solution. Hence, in this
section, we resort to an alternate approach in which we only modify the AM (Π_{AM}).
In this section (and the next), given a DeLP3E program $\mathscr{I} = (\Pi_{EM}, \Pi_{AM}, af)$, with
$\Pi_{AM} = \Omega \cup \Theta \cup \Delta \cup \Phi$, we are interested in solving the problem of incorporating
an epistemic input (f, af') into $\mathscr{I}$, where f is either an atom or a rule and af' is
equivalent to af, except for its expansion to include f. For ease of presentation, we
assume that f is to be incorporated as a fact or strict rule, as incorporating defeasible
knowledge can never lead to inconsistency since any contradicting presumption can
be defeated by each other, and hence presumptions can rule out each other. As we
are only conducting Π_{AM} revisions, for $\mathscr{I} = (\Pi_{EM}, \Pi_{AM}, af)$ and input (f, af') we
denote the revision as follows: $\mathscr{I} \bullet (f, af') = (\Pi_{EM}, \Pi'_{AM}, af')$ where Π'_{AM} is the
revised argumentation model.

   We also slightly abuse notation for the sake of presentation, as well as introduce
notation to convert sets of worlds to/from formulas:

- $\mathscr{I} \cup (f, af')$ to denote $\mathscr{I}' = (\Pi_{EM}, \Pi_{AM} \cup \{f\}, af')$.
- $(f, af') \in \mathscr{I} = (\Pi_{AM}, \Pi_{EM}, af)$ to denote $f \in \Pi_{AM}$ and $af = af'$.
- $\mathscr{W}^0_{EM}(\mathscr{I}) = \{w \in \mathscr{W}_{EM} \mid \Pi^{\mathscr{I}}_{AM}(w) \text{ is inconsistent}\}$
- $\mathscr{W}^1_{EM}(\mathscr{I}) = \{w \in \mathscr{W}^0_{EM} \mid \exists Pr \text{ s.t. } Pr \models \Pi_{EM} \wedge Pr(w) > 0\}$

Intuitively, the set $\mathscr{W}^0_{EM}(\mathscr{I})$ contains all the EM worlds for a given program
where the corresponding knowledge base in the AM is classically inconsistent and
$\mathscr{W}^1_{EM}(\mathscr{I})$ is a subset of these that can be assigned a non-zero probability—the latter
are the worlds where inconsistency in the AM can arise.

4.2.2.1 Postulates for AM-Based Belief Revision

We now analyze the rationality postulates for non-prioritized revision of belief bases
first introduced in [7] and generalized in [5], in the context of AM-based belief
revision of DeLP3E programs.

AM Inclusion For $\mathscr{I} \bullet (f, af') = (\Pi_{EM}, \Pi'_{AM}, af')$, $\Pi'_{AM} \subseteq \Pi_{AM} \cup \{f\}$.
This postulate states that the revised AM knowledge base is a subset of the union of
the original AM knowledge base and the input.

AM Vacuity If $\mathscr{I} \cup (f, af')$ is consistent, then $\mathscr{I} \bullet (f, af') \subseteq \mathscr{I} \cup (f, af')$
If simply adding the input does not cause inconsistency, then the revision operator
does precisely that.

AM Consistency Preservation If $\mathscr{I}$ is consistent, then $\mathscr{I} \bullet (f, af')$ must also be
consistent.
The operator maintains a consistent program.

AM Weak Success If $\mathscr{I} \cup (f, af')$ is consistent, then $(f, af') \in \mathscr{I} \bullet (f, af')$.
Whenever the simple addition of the input does not cause inconsistencies to arise, the result will contain the input.
If a portion of the AM knowledge base is removed by the operator, then there exists a subset of the remaining knowledge base that is not consistent with the removed element and f.

AM Pertinence For $\mathscr{I} \bullet (f, af') = (\Pi_{EM}, \Pi'_{AM}, af')$, where $\Pi'_{AM} = \Theta' \cup \Omega' \cup \Phi' \cup \Delta'$, for each $g \in \Theta \cup \Omega \setminus \Pi'_{AM}$ there exists $Y_g \supseteq \Theta' \cup \Omega' \cup \{f\}$ s.t. Y_g is consistent and $Y_g \cup \{g\}$ is inconsistent.
If a portion of the AM knowledge base is removed by the operator, then there exists a superset of the remaining knowledge base that is not consistent with the removed element and f.

AM Uniformity 1 Let $(f, af'_1), (g, af'_2)$ be two inputs where $\mathscr{W}^I_{EM}(\mathscr{I} \cup (f, af'_1)) = \mathscr{W}^I_{EM}(\mathscr{I} \cup (g, af'_2))$; for all $X \subseteq \Theta \cup \Omega$; if $X \cup \{f\}$ is inconsistent iff $X \cup \{g\}$ is inconsistent, then:

$$\Theta'_1 \cup \Omega'_1 \setminus \{f\} = \Theta'_2 \cup \Omega'_2 \setminus \{g\}$$

where $\mathscr{I} \bullet (f, af'_1) = (\Pi_{EM}, \Pi_{AM'_1}, af'_1)$ and $\mathscr{I} \bullet (g, af'_2) = (\Pi_{EM}, \Pi_{AM'_2}, af'_2)$ and $\Pi_{AM'_i} = \Theta'_i \cup \Omega'_i \cup \Phi'_i \cup \Delta'_i$.
If two inputs result in the same set of EM worlds leading to inconsistencies in an AM knowledge base, and the consistency between analogous subsets (when joined with the respective input) are the same, then the remaining elements in the AM knowledge base are the same.

AM Uniformity 2 Let $(f, af'_1), (g, af'_2)$ be two inputs where $\mathscr{W}^I_{EM}(\mathscr{I} \cup (f, af'_1)) = \mathscr{W}^I_{EM}(\mathscr{I} \cup (g, af'_2))$; for all $X \subseteq \Theta \cup \Omega$; if $X \cup \{f\}$ is inconsistent iff $X \cup \{g\}$ is inconsistent, then:

$$(\Theta \cup \Omega) \setminus (\Theta'_1 \cup \Omega'_1) = (\Theta \cup \Omega) \setminus (\Theta'_2 \cup \Omega'_2)$$

where $\mathscr{I} \bullet (f, af'_1) = (\Pi_{EM}, \Pi_{AM'_1}, af'_1)$ and $\mathscr{I} \bullet (g, af'_2) = (\Pi_{EM}, \Pi_{AM'_2}, af'_2)$ and $\Pi_{AM'_i} = \Theta'_i \cup \Omega'_i \cup \Phi'_i \cup \Delta'_i$.
If two inputs result in the same set of EM worlds leading to inconsistencies in an AM knowledge base, and the consistency between analogous subsets (when joined with the respective input) are the same, then the removed elements in the AM knowledge base are the same.

We can show an equivalence between the Uniformity postulates under certain conditions.

Proposition 4.2 *For operator $\bullet$ where for program $\mathscr{I} \bullet (f, af') = (\Pi_{EM}, \Pi'_{AM}, af')$ and $\Pi'_{AM} \subseteq \Pi_{AM} \cup \{f\}$, we have that $\bullet$ satisfies AM Uniformity 1 iff it also satisfies AM Uniformity 2.*

4.2.2.2 AM-Based Revision Operators

In this section, we define a class of operators that satisfies all of the AM rationality postulates of the previous section. We also show that there are no operators outside this class that satisfy all of the postulates.

First, we introduce notation $CandPgm_{AM}(\mathscr{I})$, which denotes a set of maximal consistent subsets of Π_{AM}. So, if $\mathscr{I}$ is consistent, then $CandPgm_{AM}(\mathscr{I}) = \{\Pi_{AM}\}$.

$$CandPgm_{AM}(\mathscr{I}) = \{\Pi'_{AM} \mid \Pi'_{AM} \subseteq \Theta \cup \Omega \text{ s.t. } \Pi'_{AM} \text{ is consistent and}$$

$$\nexists \Pi''_{AM} \subseteq \Theta \cup \Omega \text{ s.t. } \Pi''_{AM} \supset \Pi'_{AM} \text{ s.t. } \Pi''_{AM} \text{ is consistent}\}$$

For our first result, we show that an operator returning any subset of an element of $CandPgm_{AM}(\mathscr{I})$ is a necessary and sufficient condition for satisfying both the Inclusion and Consistency Preservation postulates.

Lemma 4.1 *Given program $\mathscr{I}$ and input (f, af'), operator $\bullet$ satisfies Inclusion and Consistency Preservation iff for $\mathscr{I} \bullet (f, af') = (\Pi_{EM}, \Pi'_{AM}, af')$, there exists an element $X \in CandPgm_{AM}(\mathscr{I} \cup (f, af'))$ s.t. $(\Theta \cup \Omega \cup \{f\}) \cap \Pi'_{AM} \subseteq X$.*

Our next result extends Lemma 4.1 by showing that elements of $\Pi_{AM} \cup \{f\}$ that are retained are also elements of $CandPgm_{AM}(\mathscr{I} \cup (f, af'))$ if and only if the operator satisfies Inclusion, Consistency Preservation, and Pertinence (simultaneously).

Lemma 4.2 *Given program $\mathscr{I}$ and input (f, af'), operator $\bullet$ satisfies Inclusion, Consistency Preservation, and Pertinence iff for $\mathscr{I} \bullet (f, af') = (\Pi_{EM}, \Pi'_{AM}, af')$, we have $(\Theta \cup \Omega \cup \{f\}) \cap \Pi'_{AM} \in CandPgm_{AM}(\mathscr{I} \cup (f, af'))$.*

To support the satisfaction of the first Uniformity postulate, we provide the following lemma that shows for a consistent program where two inputs cause inconsistencies to arise in the same way, that the set of candidate replacement programs (minus the added AM formula) is the same.

Lemma 4.3 *Let $\mathscr{I} = (\Pi_{EM}, \Pi_{AM}, af)$ be a consistent program, (f_1, af'_1), (f_2, af'_2) be two inputs, and $\mathscr{I}_i = (\Pi_{EM}, \Pi_{AM} \cup \{f_i\}, af'_i)$. If $\mathscr{W}^I_{EM}(\mathscr{I}_1) = \mathscr{W}^I_{EM}(\mathscr{I}_2)$, then for all $X \subseteq \Theta \cup \Omega$ we have that:*

1. *If $X \cup \{f_1\}$ is inconsistent $\Leftrightarrow$ $X \cup \{f_2\}$ is inconsistent, then:*
   $\{X \setminus \{f_1\} \mid X \in CandPgm_{AM}(\mathscr{I}_1)\} = \{X \setminus \{f_2\} \mid X \in CandPgm_{AM}(\mathscr{I}_2)\}$.
2. *If $\{X \setminus \{f_1\} \mid X \in CandPgm_{AM}(\mathscr{I}_1)\} = \{X \setminus \{f_2\} \mid X \in CandPgm_{AM}(\mathscr{I}_2)\}$ then $X \cup \{f_1\}$ is inconsistent $\Leftrightarrow$ $X \cup \{f_2\}$ is inconsistent.*

We now define the class of AM-based Operators, denoted **AMO**. Essentially, this operator selects one of the candidate programs in a deterministic fashion.

Definition 4.1 (AM-Based Operators) A belief revision operator $\bullet$ is an "AM-based" operator ($\bullet \in$ **AMO**) iff given program $\mathscr{I} = (\Pi_{EM}, \Pi_{AM}, af)$ and input (f, af'), the revision is defined as $\mathscr{I} \bullet (f, af') = (\Pi_{EM}, \Pi'_{AM}, af')$, where $\Pi'_{AM} \in CandPgm_{AM}(\mathscr{I} \cup (f, af'))$.

Finally, we are able to prove our representation theorem for AM-based belief revision. This theorem follows directly from the results presented in this section.

Theorem 4.1 (AM Representation Theorem) *An operator • belongs to class* **AMO** *iff it satisfies Inclusion, Vacuity, Consistency Preservation, Weak Success, Pertinence, and Uniformity 1.*

Example 4.3 Recall the AM knowledgebase from Fig. 3.1 and $\mathcal{K}_{EM}$ defined in Example 3.2, and suppose we would like to add $\theta_{3a} = l$ and $\theta_{3b} = \neg l$ to the AM.

Let $af(\theta_{3a}) = a$ and $af(\theta_{3a}) = b$; the input is then of the form $(f, af') = (\{\theta_{3a}, \theta_{3b}\}, af')$, where af' is the new annotation function. The program $\mathcal{I} \cup (f, af') = (\Pi_{EM}, \Pi_{AM} \cup \{f\}, af')$ will be inconsistent because of f_8. The AM-based belief revision $\mathcal{I} \bullet (f, af')$ has the option of removing θ_{3a} or θ_{3b} to recover consistency. ∎

4.2.3 Annotation Function-Based Belief Revision

In this section we attack the belief revision problem from a different angle: adjusting the annotation function. The advantage to changing the annotation function is that we might not need to discard an entire fact or strict rule from the argumentation model. Consider the following example.

Example 4.4 Let us consider two contradictory facts in an AM: a and $\neg a$ such that $af(a) = q \wedge r$ and $af(\neg a) = r \wedge s$. If we assume that q, r, s are the only atoms in the EM, then we know that a occurs under the environmental worlds $\{q, r\}$ and $\{q, r, s\}$, and that $\neg a$ occurs under the environmental worlds $\{r, s\}$ $\{q, r, s\}$.

Clearly, they cannot both be true in world $\{q, r, s\}$. Hence, a new annotation formula af' where $af'(a) = q \wedge r$ and $af'(\neg a) = r \wedge s \wedge \neg for(\{q, r, s\})$ easily solves the conflict (note that $for(w)$ specifies a formula satisfied by exactly world w). Note that we did not have to remove $\neg a$ from the knowledge base, which means that this information is not completely lost. In other word, the main difference between the AM-based belief revision and adjusting the Annotation function is that the later model allows more delicate changes to be made in order to preserve the information gathered in AM. ∎

We also note that modifications of the annotation function can be viewed as a generalization of AM modification. Consider the following:

Example 4.5 Consider again the present facts a and $\neg a$ in the AM. Assuming that this causes an inconsistency (that is, there is at least one world in which they both hold), one way to resolve it would be to remove one of these two literals. Suppose $\neg a$ is removed; this would be equivalent to setting $af(\neg a) = \bot$ (where $\bot$ represents a contradiction in the language of the EM). ∎

In this section, we introduce a set of postulates for reasoning about annotation function-based belief revision. As in the previous section, we then go on to provide a class of operators that satisfy all the postulates and show that this class includes all operators satisfying the postulates.

As in this section we are only conducting annotation function revisions, for $\mathscr{I} = (\Pi_{EM}, \Pi_{AM}, af)$ and input (f, af') we denote the revision as follows: $\mathscr{I} \blacklozenge (f, af') = (\Pi_{EM}, \Pi'_{AM}, af'')$ where $\Pi'_{AM} = \Pi_{AM} \cup \{f\}$ and af'' is the revised annotation function. Further, in this section, we often refer to "removing elements of Π_{AM}" to refer to changes to the annotation function that cause certain elements of the Π_{AM} to not have their annotations satisfied in certain EM worlds. Further, as we are looking to change the annotation function for a specific subset of facts and strict rules, we specify these subsets with the following notation.

- $wld(f) = \{w \mid w \models f\}$—the set of worlds that satisfy formula f; and
- $for(w) = \bigwedge_{a \in w} a \wedge \bigwedge_{a \notin w} \neg a$—the formula that has w as its only model.
- $\Pi^{\mathscr{I}}_{AM}(w) = \{f \in \Theta \cup \Omega \mid w \models af(f)\}$

Intuitively, $\Pi^{\mathscr{I}}_{AM}(w)$ is the subset of facts and strict rules in Π_{AM} whose annotations are true in EM world w.

4.2.3.1 Postulates for Revising the Annotation Function

Just as we did for AM-based belief revision, here we introduce rationality postulates for annotation function based belief revision. We note that except for vacuity, consistency preservation, and weak success, the postulates are defined in a different manner from the AM postulates. *The key difference between the AM-based and the AF-based postulates is that AF postulates consider subsets of the AM that occur in certain the environmental conditions—as opposed to considering the entire analytical model as a whole.* In this way, the AF-based postulates will give rise to a more fine-grained revision of the overall knowledgebase than the more coarse-grain AM-based approach.

AF Inclusion For $\mathscr{I} \blacklozenge (f, af') = (\Pi_{EM}, \Pi_{AM} \cup \{f\}, af'')$, $\forall g \in \Pi_{AM}$, we have that $wld(af''(g)) \subseteq wld(af'(g))$.
This postulate states that, for any element in the AM, the worlds that satisfy its annotation after the revision are a subset of the original set of worlds satisfying the annotation for that element.

AF Vacuity If $\mathscr{I} \cup (f, af')$ is consistent, then $\mathscr{I} \blacklozenge (f, af') \subseteq \mathscr{I} \cup (f, af')$.
This is the same as for the AM version of the postulate: no change is made if the program is consistent with the added input.

AF Consistency Preservation If $\mathscr{I}$ is consistent, then $\mathscr{I} \blacklozenge (f, af')$ must also be consistent.
Again, as with the AM version, the operator maintains a consistent program.

AF Weak Success If $\mathscr{I} \cup (f, af')$ is consistent, then $(f, af') \in \mathscr{I} \blacklozenge (f, af')$.

Whenever the input does not cause inconsistencies, it must be contained in the revised program.

For a given EM world, if a portion of the associated AM knowledge base is removed by the operator, then there exists a subset of the remaining knowledge base that is not consistent with the removed element and f.

AF Pertinence For $\mathscr{I} \blacklozenge (f, af') = (\Pi_{EM}, \Pi_{AM} \cup \{f\}, af'')$, for each $w \in \mathscr{W}_{EM}^I(\mathscr{I} \cup (f, af'))$, we have $X_w = \{h \in \Theta \cup \Omega \mid w \models af''(h)\}$; for each $g \in \Pi_{AM}(w) \setminus X_w$ there exists $Y_w \supseteq X_w \cup \{f\}$ s.t. Y_w is consistent and $Y_w \cup \{g\}$ is inconsistent.

For a given EM world, if a portion of the associated AM knowledge base is removed by the operator, then there exists a superset of the remaining knowledge base that is not consistent with the removed element and f.

AF Uniformity 1 Let $(f, af'_1), (g, af'_2)$ be two inputs where $\mathscr{W}_{EM}^I(\mathscr{I} \cup (f, af'_1)) = \mathscr{W}_{EM}^I(\mathscr{I} \cup (g, af'_2))$; for all $w \in \mathscr{W}_{EM}^I(\mathscr{I} \cup (f, af'))$ and for all $X \subseteq \Pi_{AM}(w)$; if $\{x \mid x \in X \cup \{f\}, w \models af'_1(x)\}$ is inconsistent iff $\{x \mid x \in X \cup \{g\}, w \models af'_2(x)\}$ is inconsistent, then for each $h \in \Pi_{AM}$, we have that:

$$\{w \in \mathscr{W}_{EM}^I(\mathscr{I} \cup (f, af'_1)) \mid w \models af'_1(h) \wedge \neg af''_1(h)\} =$$

$$\{w \in \mathscr{W}_{EM}^I(\mathscr{I} \cup (g, af'_2)) \mid w \models af'_2(h) \wedge \neg af''_2(h)\}.$$

If two inputs result in the same set of EM worlds leading to inconsistencies in an AM knowledge base, and the consistency between analogous subsets (when joined with the respective input) are the same, then the models removed from the annotation of a given strict rule or fact are the same for both inputs.

AF Uniformity 2 Let $(f, af'_1), (g, af'_2)$ be two inputs where $\mathscr{W}_{EM}^I(\mathscr{I} \cup (f, af'_1)) = \mathscr{W}_{EM}^I(\mathscr{I} \cup (g, af'_2))$; for all $w \in \mathscr{W}_{EM}^I(\mathscr{I} \cup (f, af'))$ and for all $X \subseteq \Pi_{AM}(w)$; if $\{x \mid x \in X \cup \{f\}, w \models af'_1(x)\}$ is inconsistent iff $\{x \mid x \in X \cup \{g\}, w \models af'_2(x)\}$ is inconsistent, then

$$\{w \in \mathscr{W}_{EM}^I(\mathscr{I} \cup (f, af'_1)) \mid w \models af'_1(h) \wedge af''_1(h)\} =$$

$$\{w \in \mathscr{W}_{EM}^I(\mathscr{I} \cup (g, af'_2)) \mid w \models af'_2(h) \wedge af''_2(h)\}.$$

If two inputs result in the same set of EM worlds leading to inconsistencies in an AM knowledge base, and the consistency between analogous subsets (when joined with the respective input) are the same, then the models retained in the annotation of a given strict rule or fact are the same for both inputs.

4.2.3.2 AF-Based Revision Operators

In this section, we introduce a class of operators for revising a DeLP3E program. Unlike the AM revision, this fine-grained approach requires an adjustment of the conditions in which elements of Π_{AM} can hold true. Hence, any subset of Π_{AM} associated with a world in $\mathscr{W}_{EM}^I(\mathscr{I} \cup (f, af'))$ must be modified by the operator in order to remain consistent. So, for such a world w, we introduce the annotation function version of the set of candidate replacement programs for $\Pi_{AM}(w)$ in order to maintain consistency and satisfy the Inclusion postulate.

$$CandPgm_{af}(w, \mathscr{I}) = \{\Pi'_{AM} \mid \Pi'_{AM} \subseteq \Pi_{AM}(w) \text{ s.t. } \Pi'_{AM} \text{ is consistent and }$$

$$\nexists \Pi''_{AM} \subseteq \Pi_{AM}(w) \text{ s.t. } \Pi''_{AM} \supset \Pi'_{AM} \text{ s.t. } \Pi''_{AM}$$

$$\text{is consistent}\}$$

Intuitively, for each world w, this is the set of is a maximal consistent subsets of $\Pi_{AM}^{\mathscr{I}}(w)$. However, unlike with AM based belief revision, the candidate replacement program are specified for specific worlds—*this in turn enables a more "surgical" adjustment to the overall knowledgebase than AM belief revision*. This is due to the fact that in AM revision, components of the analytical model are deemed to no longer hold in *any* world as opposed to a specific subset of worlds.

Before introducing our operator, we define some preliminary notation. Let Φ : $\mathscr{W}_{EM} \rightarrow 2^{[\Theta] \cup [\Omega]}$. Recall that the sets of all facts and strict rules are denoted with Θ and Ω, respectively. For each formula h in $\Pi_{AM} \cup \{f\}$, where f is part of the input, we define:

$$newFor(h, \Phi, \mathscr{I}, (f, af')) = af'(h) \wedge \bigwedge_{w \in \mathscr{W}_{EM}^I(\mathscr{I} \cup (f, af')) \mid h \notin \Phi(w)} \neg for(w)$$

Intuitively, *newFor* eliminates the inconsistency (arising from the addition of input f to the existing program $\mathscr{I}$) by adding the negation of the formulas whose only models are the inconsistent words—essentially, such models are then removed from the old formula. These inconsistent worlds are.

Now we define the class of operators called **AFO**. We show that membership in **AFO** is a necessary and sufficient condition for satisfying all postulates introduced in this chapter.

Definition 4.2 (AF-Based Operators) A belief revision operator $\blacklozenge$ is an "annotation function-based" (or af-based) operator ($\blacklozenge \in$ **AFO**) iff given program $\mathscr{I} = (\Pi_{EM}, \Pi_{AM}, af)$ and input (f, af'), the revision is then defined as $\mathscr{I} \blacklozenge (f, af') = (\Pi_{EM}, \Pi_{AM} \cup \{f\}, af'')$, where:

$$\forall h, af''(h) = newFor(h, \Phi, \mathscr{I}, (f, af'))$$

where $\forall w \in \mathscr{W}_{EM}$, $\Phi(w) \in CandPgm_{af}(w, \mathscr{I} \cup (f, af'))$.

Theorem 4.2 (Annotation Function Representation Theorem) *An operator $\blacklozenge$ belongs to class **AFO** iff it satisfies Inclusion, Vacuity, Consistency Preservation, Weak Success, Pertinence, and Uniformity 1.*

4.3 Quantitative Belief Revision Operators

We now propose exploring a novel class of operators that focus on quantitative aspects of belief revision; in the DeLP3E setting, this means measuring aspects such as the impact that revisions have on the probabilities with which literals are warranted. We will adopt the following as a running example.

Example 4.6 We consider the capture-the-flag scenario in which teams launch cyber attacks against each other in an attack-defense style competition. We use examples discussed in Chap. 2 to illustrate key concepts in this section.

Figure 4.1 shows the predicates that we will use throughout the chapter in the running example.

As shown in the figure (and discussed in more detail below), some of these predicates comprise the analytical model (AM), while others are part of the environmental model (EM). For instance, in our example, predicates stating the use of exploits as well as the teams that used the exploit in an attack such as robot mafia and apt8, are part of the analytical model. On the other hand, the environmental model contains predicates that are associated with uncertain events, such as false negatives coming up when attributing to see whether the team blue lotus was attacked by robot mafia.   ■

$\mathbf{P}_{EM}$: *robot_risk*	The attack on the team *blue lotus* falls in the category of attacks targeted by the team *robot mafia*.	
apt8_risk	The attack on the team *blue lotus* falls in the category of attacks targeted by the team *apt8*.	
FN-robot_test	Event associated with a false negative coming up when attributing to see whether *blue lotus* was attacked by *robot mafia*.	
FN-pwnies	Event associated with a false negative coming up when attributing to see whether *blue lotus* was attacked by *pwnies*.	
$\mathbf{P}_{AM}$: *exploit_X*	The team *blue lotus* was targeted using *exploit X*.	
exploit_Y	The team *blue lotus* was targeted using *exploit Y*.	
exploit_Z	The team *blue lotus* was targeted using *exploit Z*.	
robot_mafia	The team *blue lotus* was targeted by a team with behavior consistent with that of *robot mafia*.	
apt8	The team *blue lotus* was targeted by a team with behavior consistent with that of *apt8*.	
samurai	The team *blue lotus* was targeted by a team with behavior consistent with that of *samurai*.	
neg_robot_mafia	Team not targeted by *robot mafia* .	
neg_pwnies	Team not targeted by *pwnies*.	
pos_apt8	Team targeted by *apt8*.	

Fig. 4.1 Explanation of the meaning of the predicates used in the running example

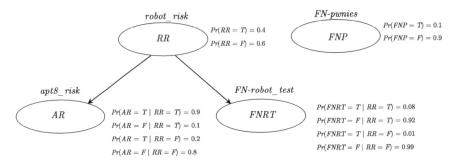

Fig. 4.2 Bayesian network used in the EM of the running example. The names of the random variables are simply the abbreviations of their corresponding atoms: $AR \mapsto robot\_risk$, $DR \mapsto apt8\_risk$, $FNAT \mapsto FN - robot\_test$, and $FNTS \mapsto FN - pwnies$

World	robot_risk	apt8_risk	FN_robot_test	FN_pwnies	Probability
λ_1	T	T	T	T	0.00288
λ_2	T	T	T	F	0.02592
λ_3	T	T	F	T	0.03312
λ_4	T	T	F	F	0.29808
λ_5	T	F	T	T	0.00032
λ_6	T	F	T	F	0.00288
λ_7	T	F	F	T	0.00368
λ_8	T	F	F	F	0.03312
λ_9	F	T	T	T	0.00048
λ_{10}	F	T	T	F	0.00432
λ_{11}	F	T	F	T	0.04752
λ_{12}	F	T	F	F	0.42768
λ_{13}	F	F	T	T	0.00012
λ_{14}	F	F	T	F	0.00108
λ_{15}	F	F	F	T	0.01188
λ_{16}	F	F	F	F	0.10692

Fig. 4.3 Probability distribution for the worlds in the running example

In the following, we use $basic_{AM}$ to denote all possible conjunctions or disjunctions of literals from $\mathbf{L}_{AM}$, which we refer to as *basic formulas*. The following is an example of a Bayesian Network over the running example.

Example 4.7 Consider the set $\mathbf{P}_{EM}$ from Fig. 4.1. The Bayesian network depicted in Fig. 4.2 describes the probability distribution Pr over all possible worlds $\mathcal{W}_{EM}$ shown in Fig. 4.3.

So, for instance, the probability that false negatives do not arise in any of the two cases, and that the team blue lotus can be attacked by both robot mafia and pwnies (world λ_4) is 0.29808. ∎

The following is an example of a PreDeLP program over the running example.

Example 4.8 Consider again the capture-the-flag scenario from our running example; the DeLP3E program in Fig. 4.4 encodes some basic knowledge that a security

$\Theta : \theta_1 = exploit\_X$
$\quad\quad \theta_2 = exploit\_Y$
$\quad\quad \theta_3 = exploit\_Z$

$\Omega : \omega_1 = \neg exploit\_X \leftarrow neg\_pwnies$
$\quad\quad \omega_2 = \neg exploit\_Y \leftarrow neg\_robot\_mafia$
$\quad\quad \omega_3 = robot\_mafia \leftarrow apt8$
$\quad\quad \omega_4 = apt8 \leftarrow pos\_apt8$

$\Phi : \emptyset$

$\Delta : \delta_1 = samurai \prec exploit\_X, apt8$
$\quad\quad \delta_2 = robot\_mafia \prec exploit\_Y$
$\quad\quad \delta_3 = apt8 \prec exploit\_X$
$\quad\quad \delta_4 = robot\_mafia \prec exploit\_Z$

Fig. 4.4 A ground argumentation framework

$\langle \mathscr{A}_1, robot\_mafia \rangle \;\; \mathscr{A}_1 = \{\theta_1, \delta_3, \omega_3\}$
$\langle \mathscr{A}_2, robot\_mafia \rangle \;\; \mathscr{A}_2 = \{\theta_3, \delta_4\}$
$\langle \mathscr{A}_3, \neg exploit\_X \rangle \;\; \mathscr{A}_3 = \{\omega_1\} \cup \{neg\_pwnies \prec\}$

Fig. 4.5 Example arguments based on the running example scenario

Fig. 4.6 An example of an annotation function over the running example

$af(\theta_1) = $ True
$af(\theta_2) = $ True
$af(\theta_3) = $ True

$af(\omega_1) = $ True $\quad\quad\quad af(\delta_1) = $ True
$af(\omega_2) = $ True $\quad\quad\quad af(\delta_2) = robot\_risk$
$af(\omega_3) = $ True $\quad\quad\quad af(\delta_3) = apt8\_risk$
$af(\omega_4) = $ True $\quad\quad\quad af(\delta_4) = robot\_risk$

analysts might use for cyber attribution. For instance, strict rule ω_1 states that based on a negative result of team pwnies being the attacker we can conclude that exploit_X was not used in the attack. On the other hand, defeasible rule δ_1 states that if exploit_X was used to target apt8, then the attacker can be samurai.   ∎

Example 4.9 Figure 4.5 shows example arguments based on the PreDeLP program from Fig. 4.4. Argument $\mathscr{A}_3$ uses an additional component not present in the original program, and states that if we can assume a negative result for pwnies being the attacker, we can conclude that exploit_X was not used in the attack.   ∎

Figure 4.6 shows an example of an annotation function for our running example; for instance, the annotation for rule δ_2 means that this rule only holds whenever the probabilistic event *robot_risk* is true. If annotations are "True", this means that they hold in all possible worlds.

$\lambda_1: \{\theta_1,\theta_2,\theta_3,$ $\omega_1,\omega_2,\omega_3,\omega_4,$ $\delta_1,\delta_2,\delta_3,\delta_4\}$	$\lambda_2: \{\theta_1,\theta_2,\theta_3,$ $\omega_1,\omega_2,\omega_3,\omega_4,$ $\delta_1,\delta_2,\delta_3,\delta_4\}$	$\lambda_3: \{\theta_1,\theta_2,\theta_3,$ $\omega_1,\omega_2,\omega_3,\omega_4,$ $\delta_1,\delta_2,\delta_3,\delta_4\}$	$\lambda_4: \{\theta_1,\theta_2,\theta_3,$ $\omega_1,\omega_2,\omega_3,\omega_4,$ $\delta_1,\delta_2,\delta_3,\delta_4\}$
$\lambda_5: \{\theta_1,\theta_2,\theta_3,$ $\omega_1,\omega_2,\omega_3,\omega_4,$ $\delta_1,\delta_2,\delta_4\}$	$\lambda_6: \{\theta_1,\theta_2,\theta_3,$ $\omega_1,\omega_2,\omega_3,\omega_4,$ $\delta_1,\delta_2,\delta_4\}$	$\lambda_7: \{\theta_1,\theta_2,\theta_3,$ $\omega_1,\omega_2,\omega_3,\omega_4,$ $\delta_1,\delta_2,\delta_4\}$	$\lambda_8: \{\theta_1,\theta_2,\theta_3,$ $\omega_1,\omega_2,\omega_3,\omega_4,$ $\delta_1,\delta_2,\delta_4\}$
$\lambda_9: \{\theta_1,\theta_2,\theta_3,$ $\omega_1,\omega_2,\omega_3,\omega_4,$ $\delta_1,\delta_3\}$	$\lambda_{10}: \{\theta_1,\theta_2,\theta_3,$ $\omega_1,\omega_2,\omega_3,\omega_4,$ $\delta_1,\delta_3\}$	$\lambda_{11}: \{\theta_1,\theta_2,\theta_3,$ $\omega_1,\omega_2,\omega_3,\omega_4,$ $\delta_1,\delta_3\}$	$\lambda_{12}: \{\theta_1,\theta_2,\theta_3,$ $\omega_1,\omega_2,\omega_3,\omega_4,$ $\delta_1,\delta_3\}$
$\lambda_{13}: \{\theta_1,\theta_2,\theta_3,$ $\omega_1,\omega_2,\omega_3,\omega_4,$ $\delta_1\}$	$\lambda_{14}: \{\theta_1,\theta_2,\theta_3,$ $\omega_1,\omega_2,\omega_3,\omega_4,$ $\delta_1\}$	$\lambda_{15}: \{\theta_1,\theta_2,\theta_3,$ $\omega_1,\omega_2,\omega_3,\omega_4,$ $\delta_1\}$	$\lambda_{16}: \{\theta_1,\theta_2,\theta_3,$ $\omega_1,\omega_2,\omega_3,\omega_4,$ $\delta_1\}$

Fig. 4.7 A depiction of how the DeLP3E program in the running example can be decomposed into one classical PreDeLP program for each possible EM world (cf. Fig. 4.3 for the definition of worlds λ_1–λ_{16} in terms of the random variables in the EM)

In the following, given DeLP3E program $\mathscr{I} = (\Pi_{EM}, \Pi_{AM}, af)$ and $\lambda \in \mathscr{W}_{EM}$, we use notation $\Pi_{AM}(\lambda) = \{f \in \Pi_{AM}$ s.t. $\lambda \models af(f)\}$. This gives rise to a *decomposed view* of DeLP3E programs, as illustrated next.

Example 4.10 Consider the different examples presented so far: the EM from Example 4.7 (with the worlds from Fig. 4.3), Π_{AM} from Fig. 4.4, the arguments in Fig. 4.5, and the annotation function from Fig. 4.6—these components give rise to a DeLP3E program $\mathscr{I} = (\Pi_{EM}, \Pi_{AM}, af)$. Figure 4.7 shows how $\mathscr{I}$ can be decomposed into one classical PreDeLP program $\Pi_{AM}(\lambda)$ for each world $\lambda \in \mathscr{W}_{EM}$.

For instance, $\Pi_{AM}(\lambda_7)$ contains θ_1, θ_2, θ_3, ω_1, ω_2, ω_3, ω_4, and δ_1 because the annotation function associates condition True to all of these components; it contains δ_2 and δ_4 because condition *robot_risk* is true in λ_7, and it does not contain δ_3 because condition *apt8_risk* is false in λ_7.   ∎

The most direct way of considering consequences of DeLP3E programs is thus to consider what happens in each world in $\mathscr{W}_{EM}$; that is, the defeat relationship among arguments depends on the current state of the (EM) world.

Example 4.11 Consider the different examples presented so far: the worlds in Fig. 4.3, Π_{AM} from Fig. 4.4, the arguments in Fig. 4.5, and the annotation function from Fig. 4.6.

Since argument $\mathscr{A}_1$ uses defeasible rule δ_3, and $af(\delta_3) = apt8\_risk$ (while the other two components have annotation "True"), we can conclude that this argument exists in worlds in which *apt8_risk* is true, i.e., λ_1–λ_4 and λ_9–λ_{12}.   ∎

Example 4.12 Let us return to the running example; consider Π_{AM} from Fig. 4.4, Π_{EM} from Fig. 4.2, and the annotation function from Fig. 4.6, with the addition of fact $\theta_4 = pos\_apt8$ with $af(\theta_4) = $ True and fact $\theta_5 = neg\_robot\_mafia$ with $af(\theta_5) = \neg FN\text{-}robot\_test$. It is now clear that the program is inconsistent, since there exists world λ_3 (among several others) such that $\bigcup_{x \in \Theta \cup \Omega \,|\, \lambda_3 \models af(x)} \{x\}$ warrants both *robot_mafia* (via argument with θ_4 and ω_3) and ¬*robot_mafia* (via argument with θ_5 and ω_2).   ∎

We have finally arrived at the main problem we address in this chapter—revising knowledge bases. This problem can be generically stated as: given DeLP3E program $\mathscr{I} = (\Pi_{EM}, \Pi_{AM}, af)$, with $\Pi_{AM} = \Omega \cup \Theta \cup \Delta \cup \Phi$ and a pair (f, af') where f is either an atom or a rule and af' is equivalent to af, except for its expansion to include $f,^1$ obtain a new program $\mathscr{I}'$ called the *revised* knowledge base that addresses the incorporation of the *epistemic input* (f, af') into the original program; we denote this operation with the symbol "•"—i.e., $\mathscr{I}' = \mathscr{I} \bullet (f, af')$.

Now, the problem statement as presented above is quite vague, since we did not give any details as to how the operator "addresses the incorporation" of the epistemic input. There are many approaches in the literature that address this problem quite differently; one of the main properties that characterize revision operators is whether or not they satisfy the *Success* property, which states that the epistemic input must be a consequence of the revised knowledge base. Here, we will adopt a cautious stance and assume that this property does not hold in general; therefore, we focus on so-called *non-prioritized* revision operators.

The basic issue that revision operators must deal with is inconsistency (we will discuss this in more depth shortly); as we saw in Sect. 3.4, inconsistency in DeLP3E programs involves worlds that have non-zero probability and an associated PreDeLP program that is inconsistent. In the previous section we identified three basic approaches that can be taken towards solving this problem: *Modifying the EM*, *Modifying the AM*, and *Modifying the annotation function*. In the following, we will assume that epistemic inputs involve only strict components (facts or rules), since defeasible components can always be added without inconsistencies arising. Regarding these three possible approaches, we now focus on the third one since it is a generalization of the second—as we saw earlier, if we only allow removing elements from the AM, such an operation will have the same effect as not removing the element but modifying the annotation function so that it associates the formula "⊥" to it. Furthermore, operations of the first kind alone do not suffice to perform revisions, as can be seen in the following simple example.

Example 4.13 Consider the following DeLP3E program, where the EM consists of two worlds $\{a\}$ and $\{\neg a\}$, each with probability 0.5:

$$
\begin{aligned}
\omega_1 &: \quad p \leftarrow q & af(\omega_1) &= a \\
\theta_1 &: \quad \neg p & af(\theta_1) &= a \\
\omega_2 &: \quad \neg p \leftarrow q & af(\omega_2) &= \neg a \\
\theta_2 &: \quad p & af(\theta_2) &= \neg a
\end{aligned}
$$

Now, suppose we wish to revise by formula $\theta_3 : q$ with $af(\theta_3) = \mathsf{True}$. Since both EM worlds are inconsistent with the formula, it is impossible to change the allocation of the probability mass in order to avoid inconsistencies; therefore, the only option is to reject the input.   ∎

---

[1] That is, $af'(x) = af(x)$ for all $x \in dom(af)$, and $dom(af') = dom(af) \cup \{f\}$.

Analytical Model	**Annotation Function**
$\Theta :$ $\theta_1 =$ *exploit_X*	True
$\theta_2 =$ *exploit_Y*	True
$\theta_3 =$ *exploit_Z*	True
$\theta_4 =$ *neg_robot_mafia*	$\{\neg FN\text{-}robot\_test\}$
$\theta_5 =$ *neg_pwnies*	$\{\neg FN\text{-}pwnies\}$
$\Omega :$ $\omega_1 =$ $\neg exploit\_X \leftarrow neg\_pwnies$	True
$\omega_2 =$ $\neg exploit\_Y \leftarrow neg\_robot\_mafia$	True
$\omega_3 =$ *robot_mafia* $\leftarrow$ *apt8*	True
$\omega_4 =$ *apt8* $\leftarrow$ *pos_apt8*	True
$\Phi :$ $\emptyset$	
$\Delta :$ $\delta_1 =$ *samurai* $\prec$ *exploit_X, apt8*	True
$\delta_2 =$ *robot_mafia* $\prec$ *exploit_Y*	$\{robot\_risk\}$
$\delta_3 =$ *apt8* $\prec$ *exploit_X*	$\{apt8\_risk\}$
$\delta_4 =$ *robot_mafia* $\prec$ *exploit_Z*	$\{robot\_risk\}$

Fig. 4.8 The DeLP3E program from the running example, after adding facts θ_4 and θ_5. The annotation function is provided in a separate column for convenience

4.3.1 Towards Quantitative Revision

Traditionally, belief revision has been addressed from a qualitative point of view rather than a quantitative one. A simple example of this is the fact that, faced with the option of removing either both atoms a and b or only atom c, classical revision operators typically declare both options to be just as good, since neither is a subset of the other; it could be argued, then, that taking quantitative aspects into account (such as the number of elements removed) *may* lead to a better solution—of course, this may depend on other factors. As we will see, there are different ways in which such quantitative aspects can be incorporated into revision operations. For instance, in our setting, DeLP3E programs can be regarded in a world-by-world manner, and changes made in one world can be compared to those made in another. The **AFO** operators described in Sect. 4.2 make decisions for each world independently; we now wish to address the issue of taking into account different kinds of quantitative aspects when revising DeLP3E programs. The following example motivates our approach in our capture-the-flag scenario.

Example 4.14 Consider again the running example, and suppose the a security analyst has decided to test who conducted the cyber attack between pwnies and robot mafia, and that both tests yielded negative results. Note that the validity of these tests is subject to probabilistic events (in this case, false negatives). The new program is reproduced in Fig. 4.8.

Figure 4.9 shows the world-by-world decomposition of the new program, and the atoms that are warranted in each case. From the information in this figure, we can

World	Probability	Warranted Literals
λ_1	0.00288	$\{\theta_1, \theta_2, \theta_3\} \cup \{apt8, \ samurai, \ robot\_mafia\}$
λ_2	0.02592	$\{\theta_1, \theta_2, \theta_3, \theta_5\} \cup \{apt8, \ \neg samurai, \ robot\_mafia\}$
λ_3	0.03312	$\{\theta_1, \theta_2, \theta_3, \theta_4\} \cup \{apt8, \ \neg samurai, \ robot\_mafia\}$
λ_4	0.29808	$\{\theta_1, \theta_2, \theta_3, \theta_4, \theta_5\} \cup \{\neg samurai, \ \neg robot\_mafia\}$
λ_5	0.00032	$\{\theta_1, \theta_2, \theta_3\} \cup \{robot\_mafia\}$
λ_6	0.00288	$\{\theta_1, \theta_2, \theta_3, \theta_5\} \cup \{\neg samurai, \ robot\_mafia\}$
λ_7	0.00368	$\{\theta_1, \theta_2, \theta_3, \theta_4\} \cup \{\neg robot\_mafia\}$
λ_8	0.03312	$\{\theta_1, \theta_2, \theta_3, \theta_4, \theta_5\} \cup \{\neg samurai, \ \neg robot\_mafia\}$
λ_9	0.00048	$\{\theta_1, \theta_2, \theta_3\} \cup \{apt8, \ samurai, \ robot\_mafia\}$
λ_{10}	0.00432	$\{\theta_1, \theta_2, \theta_3, \theta_5\} \cup \{apt8, \ \neg samurai, \ robot\_mafia\}$
λ_{11}	0.04752	$\{\theta_1, \theta_2, \theta_3, \theta_4\} \cup \{samurai, \ \neg robot\_mafia\}$
λ_{12}	0.42768	$\{\theta_1, \theta_2, \theta_3, \theta_4, \theta_5\} \cup \{\neg samurai, \ \neg robot\_mafia\}$
λ_{13}	0.00012	$\{\theta_1, \theta_2, \theta_3\}$
λ_{14}	0.00108	$\{\theta_1, \theta_2, \theta_3, \theta_5\} \cup \{\neg samurai\}$
λ_{15}	0.01188	$\{\theta_1, \theta_2, \theta_3, \theta_4\} \cup \{\neg robot\_mafia\}$
λ_{16}	0.10692	$\{\theta_1, \theta_2, \theta_3, \theta_4, \theta_5\} \cup \{\neg robot\_mafia, \ \neg samurai\}$

Fig. 4.9 Atoms that are warranted in each possible EM world, given the AM and annotation function in Fig. 4.8

compute the following probabilities for the hypotheses that the security analyst is contemplating the teams (apt8, robot mafia, samurai):

Literal	Probability
apt8	: 0.06672
samurai	: 0.05088
¬samurai	: 0.93324
robot_mafia	: 0.06992
¬robot_mafia	: 0.92888

Since they all have low probabilities after performing the tests, the analyst decides to test for team apt8 and in this case receives a positive result (atom *pos_apt8*). For the sake of this example, we will assume that the validity of the outcome of this test (unlike the other two) is not subject to probabilistic events—thus, we have $af(pos\_apt8) = \mathsf{True}$.

Now, while for the first two tests we were able to simply add the corresponding atoms and extend the annotation function accordingly, simply adding $\theta_6 = pos\_apt8$ with $af(\theta_6) = \mathsf{True}$ causes inconsistencies to arise in eight of the possible worlds ($\lambda_3, \lambda_4, \lambda_7, \lambda_8, \lambda_{11}, \lambda_{12}, \lambda_{15}$, and λ_{16}). Essentially, the problems arise because the negative robot mafia test allows us to conclude that team robot mafia was not the attacker, while the positive apt8 test would allow us to conclude that indeed team apt8 was the attacker. Since both derivations only involve strict components, this leads to an inconsistent AM.   ∎

Example 4.14 shows an interesting case of belief revision in DeLP3E programs; when presented with new information that is in conflict with existing one, we must find a way to address its incorporation into the existing knowledge—non-prioritized operators are very flexible, since they always have the option of ignoring the new information. However, this flexibility also means that—in the case of DeLP3E programs—there is no guidance with respect to how revisions should be carried out *globally*, since each world is treated as a separate revision problem. Next, we discuss two kinds of functions that will prove to be useful in addressing this situation.

4.3.2 Two Building Blocks

We now introduce warrant probability functions and revision objective functions, which are later used in the definition of our new class of non-prioritized belief revision operators.

Warrant Probability Functions   As one of the building blocks to our quantitative approach, given a DeLP3E program $\mathscr{I}$ we define *warrant probability functions* (WPFs, for short).

Before introducing these formulas, we need to present a simple extension to the concept of "warrant status", which is up to now defined for literals. The following definition is a simple extension to conjunctions or disjunctions of literals.

Definition 4.3 (Warranting a Conjunction/Disjunction of Literals)   Let Π_{AM} be a ground PreDeLP program and Q be either a conjunction or disjunction of ground literals $L_1, \ldots, L_n$. The *warrant status* of Q with respect to Π_{AM} is defined as follows:

1. If Q is a single literal L, then the warrant status of Q is the warrant status of L in Π_{AM}.
2. If $Q = Q_1 \wedge Q_2$ then the warrant status of Q is:

   - *Yes* iff the warrant status of both Q_1 and Q_2 is *Yes*;
   - *No* if the warrant status of either Q_1 or Q_2 is *No*; and
   - *Undecided* whenever neither of the above cases hold.

3. If $Q = Q_1 \vee Q_2$ then the warrant status of Q is:

   - *Yes* iff the warrant status of either Q_1 or Q_2 is *Yes*;
   - *No* if the warrant status of both Q_1 and Q_2 is *No*; and
   - *Undecided* whenever neither of the above cases hold.

Using Definition 4.3, we can easily extend the *nec* and *poss* notations (cf. Page 32) to conjunctions and disjunctions of literals.

The following result is a consequence of the fact that conflicting literals cannot be warranted in (Pre)DeLP [6].

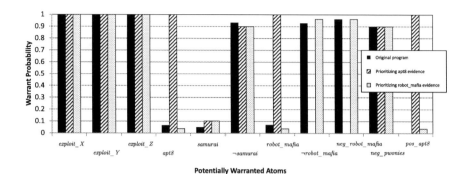

Fig. 4.10 Histogram depiction of the entailment probability functions for the programs discussed in Example 4.14

Proposition 4.3 *Let Π_{AM} be a ground PreDeLP program and $Q = L_1 \wedge \ldots \wedge L_n$ be a conjunction of ground literals. Then, only one of the following cases holds: (i) $P \vdash_{war} Q$, (ii) $P \vdash_{war} \neg Q$, or (iii) the warrant status of Q is undecided.*

Warrant Probability Functions are then simply defined as partial mappings with signature:

$$\Upsilon_{\mathscr{I}} : basic_{AM} \to [0, 1]$$

such that for $f \in basic_{AM}$, $\Upsilon_{\mathscr{I}}(f) = p$ if and only if $\sum_{\lambda \in nec(f)} Pr(\lambda) = p.$[2] When the program is clear from context, we drop the subscript and write simply Υ. In the following, we use notation $dom(\Upsilon)$ to denote the set of formulas for which Υ is defined. The table shown in Example 4.14 is a simple example of a WPF, whose domain is a handful of literals. The following is another example along the same vein.

Example 4.15 Figure 4.10 shows three examples of WPFs in which the domains are fixed to the set of literals that can be warranted in the input program. These functions are related to the revision described in Example 4.14: the black bars show the original probabilities, the striped bars give the probabilities yielded by the program obtained by favoring the inclusion of the positive apt8 test, while the light gray bars depict the probabilities obtained by favoring the negative robot mafia test. Figure 4.11 shows the three revised programs. ∎

---

[2]Note that this definition can easily be extended to deal with probability intervals as well (i.e., using both *nec* and *poss*); here, for simplicity of presentation, we adopt this definition in order to work with point probabilities.

Analytical Model	af_1	af_2	af_3
$\Theta:\ \theta_1 =\ exploit\_X$	True	True	True
$\theta_2 =\ exploit\_Y$	True	True	True
$\theta_3 =\ exploit\_Z$	True	True	True
$\theta_4 =\ neg\_robot\_mafia$	$\neg FN\text{-}robot\_test$	False	$af_1(\theta_4)$
$\theta_5 =\ neg\_pwnies$	$\neg FN\text{-}pwnies$	$af_1(\theta_5)$	$af_1(\theta_5)$
$\theta_6 =\ pos\_apt8\_test$	True	True	$\neg af_1(\theta_4)$
$\Omega:\ \omega_1 = \neg exploit\_X \leftarrow$			
$\qquad\qquad neg\_pwnies$	True	True	True
$\omega_2 = \neg exploit\_Y \leftarrow neg\_robot\_mafia$	True	True	True
$\omega_3 =\ robot\_mafia \leftarrow apt8$	True	True	True
$\omega_4 =\ apt8 \leftarrow pos\_apt8$	True	True	True
$\Phi:\ \emptyset$			
$\Delta:\ \delta_1 =\ samurai \prec$			
$\qquad\qquad exploit\_X, apt8$	True	True	True
$\delta_2 =\ robot\_mafia \prec exploit\_Y$	$\{apt8\_risk\}$	$af_1(\delta_2)$	$af_1(\delta_2)$
$\delta_3 =\ apt8 \prec exploit\_X$	$\{apt8\_risk\}$	$af_1(\delta_3)$	$af_1(\delta_3)$
$\delta_4 =\ robot\_mafia \prec exploit\_Z$	$\{robot\_risk\}$	$af_1(\delta_4)$	$af_1(\delta_4)$

Fig. 4.11 The DeLP3E program from the running example, after performing three revisions: (i) The addition of the θ_4 and θ_5, as discussed in Example 4.14; (ii) The revision by pos_apt8 by prioritizing this input; and (iii) The same revision but prioritizing neg_robot_mafia

Revision Objective Functions The other building block allows us to effectively quantify *how good* a revision is considered to be. Towards this end, we define *revision objective functions* (ROFs, for short) as functions that take two DeLP3E programs $\mathscr{I}_1$ and $\mathscr{I}_2$, along with an epistemic input (f, af), and returns a positive real number. We keep the definition of ROFs very general in order to allow different kinds of objectives to be specified. The following is a simple example of a ROF over our running example, which makes use of warranting probability functions.

Example 4.16 Let us return once again to the capture-the-flag example. Suppose that we take the three revised programs we presented (Fig. 4.11)—call them $\mathscr{I}_1$, $\mathscr{I}_2$, and $\mathscr{I}_3$—and that we wish to compare them with respect to the effect of the last revision over the warranted atoms, taking the probabilities yielded by $\mathscr{I}_1$ as the baseline. So, we define the following revision objective function:

$$\Psi(\mathscr{I}, \mathscr{I}', (f, af')) = e^{-\sum_{L \in L_{AM}, L \neq f} |\Upsilon_{\mathscr{I}}(L) - \Upsilon_{\mathscr{I}'}(L)|}$$

where $\Upsilon_{\mathscr{I}}$ is the WPF for program $\mathscr{I}$.

Intuitively, this function sums up all the differences between the probabilities of literals entailed by the programs, but ignores the input (if it is a literal). In this way, a *distance* between the original program and the two possible revisions is obtained based on the effects that each revision had on the probabilities with which literals are derived. So, for our revisions, we get:

$$\Psi(\mathscr{I}_1, \mathscr{I}_2, (pos\_apt8, af_2)) \approx 0.0547$$
$$\Psi(\mathscr{I}_1, \mathscr{I}_3, (pos\_apt8, af_3)) \approx 0.8611$$

Therefore, we can conclude that the revision yielding $\mathscr{I}_3$ is preferred over the one yielding $\mathscr{I}_2$ when this ROF is adopted.   ∎

Note that the function presented in Example 4.16 is just one possibility; the framework is very flexible and allows the user to express many different functions, depending on the specific way in which they wish to express distances between the original program and a given revised program.

4.3.3 The Class **QAFO**

Given the basic constructs introduced above, we can now define the class of *quantitative* annotation function-based revision operators.

Definition 4.4 (The Class QAFO) Let $\mathscr{I} = (\Pi_{EM}, \Pi_{AM}, af)$, with $\Pi_{AM} = \Omega \cup \Theta \cup \Delta \cup \Phi$ be a DeLP3E program, $\star \in$ **AFO** be an annotation function-based belief revision operator, and Ψ be a revision objective function. Operator $\star$ is said to be a *quantitative af-based* operator (denoted $\star \in$ **QAFO**) if:

> Given an epistemic input (f, af'), we have that if $\mathscr{I}' = \mathscr{I} \star (f, af')$ then there does not exist DeLP3E program $\mathscr{I}'' = \mathscr{I} \bullet (f, af')$ such that $\Psi(\mathscr{I}, \mathscr{I}'', (f, af')) > \Psi(\mathscr{I}, \mathscr{I}', (f, af'))$,

where $\bullet \in$ **AFO** is an arbitrary operator.

So, this subclass of **AFO** simply takes a revision objective function and uses it to obtain the best possible revised program. We present a second example, based on our previous work on applications of DeLP3E to problems in the cybersecurity domain [9], shows how **QAFO** operators can be applied to belief revision problems.

Example 4.17 Suppose we are modeling a cybersecurity scenario in which a computer worm has been deployed and has infected millions of computers worldwide—by the time the worm is discovered, it is very difficult to reason about the origin and even the intended target of the attack.

Towards this end, we can model all knowledge available by means of a DeLP3E program as discussed in Sect. 3.5: $\mathscr{I} = (\Pi_{EM}, \Pi_{AM}, af)$, in which there is one distinguished predicate $condOp(A, O)$ in the AM that is intuitively read as "actor A conducted operation O". Furthermore, if we assume that only one actor is ever responsible for an operation (an assumption that can easily be removed), we have an integrity constraint of the form $oneOf(C)$, where C is the set of all ground atoms built with the *condOp* predicate.

Given this setup, we can define a WPF with a domain consisting of some formulas of interest that reflect conditions that the analysts would like to remain relatively unaffected when incorporating new information. For instance, suppose we define:

$$dom(\Upsilon) = \Big\{ \neg condOp(countryA, worm) \wedge \neg condOp(countryB, worm)$$

$$condOp(countryD, worm)\Big\},$$

denoting the fact that neither country A nor country B are responsible for deploying the worm, and that country D is. If we pair this WPF with the ROF from Example 4.16, the corresponding **QAFO** operator will prefer revisions that do not affect the conclusions already reached regarding the probabilities assigned to these statements.

In other words, this definition of $dom(\Upsilon)$, with the ROF in question, causes distances to be gauged relative to their effect on the probabilities assigned to the suspicions that (i) neither country A nor country B carried out the attack, and (ii) country D is behind the attack. Thus, such a setup causes the operator to prefer revisions that keep the probabilities assigned to such suspicions as close as possible to the ones yielded by the original program.   ∎

In the next section, we study the computational complexity associated with this approach to belief revision in the DeLP3E setting.

4.3.4   *Computational Complexity*

In this section, we will focus on some of the computational aspects of quantitative af-based belief revision operations.

As a first observation, we have that the problem of deciding the warranting status in a (classical) PreDeLP program has not yet been pinpointed. In [2], the authors present a proof for the PSPACE-completeness of the problem of marking a *given* dialectical tree; PSPACE membership for deciding the warrant status is therefore a direct consequence of this result, since a dialectical tree can be built within this budget. As a step towards finding a lower bound for the complexity of the problem in general, we have the following.

Proposition 4.4 *Let Π_{AM} be a ground PreDeLP program and L be a ground literal. Deciding $\Pi_{AM} \vdash_{war} L$ is NP-hard.*

As a corollary to Proposition 4.4, we have that deciding our extended notion of warrant status remains within the same complexity bounds.

Corollary 4.1 *Let Π_{AM} be a ground PreDeLP program and Q be either a conjunction or disjunction of ground literals. Deciding $\Pi_{AM} \vdash_{war} Q$ is NP-hard and in PSPACE.*

Assumption Since, as stated above, the precise complexity of deciding the warrant status of a literal in a PreDeLP program is not yet known, and with the objective of separating the complexity of this problem from the complexity of the problems inherent to quantitative belief revision in DeLP3E programs, in the following we will make the assumption that classical warranting in PreDeLP is decidable in polynomial time. This is not an unreasonable assumption if we consider the possibility of pre-compiling inferences [1] or having tractable approximation algorithms to address the problem. We call this the *polynomial-time warranting* (*PTW*) assumption. Note that, even though this assumption does not hold in general, it is a useful tool in the analysis of the complexity of the problems studied here; it is also with this spirit that we make use of the PTW assumption.

Unfortunately, our first result regarding the probabilistic extension of PreDeLP tells us that computing WPFs runs into a computational tractability hurdle.

Theorem 4.3 *Under the PTW assumption, computing the warrant probability function for a DeLP3E program is #P-hard.*

The complexity class #P contains problems related to *counting* solutions (or, in Turing machine terms, accepting paths) to problems in NP. The decision version of this class is called PP, and contains problems decidable by a probabilistic Turing machine in polynomial time, with error probability less than a certain proportion (say, 1/2). Unfortunately, Toda's theorem [12] tells us that a polynomial-time Turing machine with either a PP or #P oracle can solve all problems in the polynomial hierarchy.

Though it might be surmised that the #P-hardness is caused solely by the computation of probabilities (as is the case in many probabilistic formalisms), the construction used in proof of Theorem 4.3 [11] allows us to arrive at the following conclusion.

Observation 2 *Computing the warrant probability function for a DeLP3E program is #P-hard even in the special case in which probabilities associated with EM worlds can be computed in PTIME.*

Though this intractability holds in general, restricting the EM can soften the impact on complexity. For instance, if we assume that Nilsson's probabilistic logic [8] is used then the complexity is lowered, as we show next; first, we introduce a key lemma:

Lemma 4.4 ([3, 4]) *If a system of m linear equalities and/or inequalities has a nonnegative solution, then it has a nonnegative solution with at most m positive variables.*

This result was first introduced in [3], and later used in [4] to show that deciding the validity of a formula in their logic is NP-complete. We can now state our result.

Proposition 4.5 *Under the PTW assumption, and assuming that Nilsson's probabilistic logic is used in the EM, computing the warrant probability function for a DeLP3E program is NP-complete.*

The previous result gives us a hint towards reaching the next one: if we combine the simplifying assumption that probabilities can be computed tractably with the further assumption that the number of EM worlds that have non-zero probability is bounded by a polynomial (Condition 1 below), then we are guaranteed that computing WPFs is also tractable.

Corollary 4.2 *Let $\mathscr{I} = (\Pi_{EM}, \Pi_{AM}, af)$, with $\Pi_{AM} = \Omega \cup \Theta \cup \Delta \cup \Phi$, be a DeLP3E program. If we make the following assumptions:*

1. *$|\{\lambda \mid \lambda \in \mathscr{W}_{EM} \text{ and } Pr(\lambda) > 0\}| \in O(poly(n))$, where n represents the size of the input;*
2. *$Pr(\lambda)$ can be computed in PTIME for any $\lambda \in \mathscr{W}_{EM}$; and*
3. *the PTW assumption holds,*

then warrant probability functions for $\mathscr{I}$ can also be computed in PTIME.

Unfortunately, the following result states that even in this scenario we still face an intractable hurdle when computing optimal revisions.

Theorem 4.4 *Let $\mathscr{I} = (\Pi_{EM}, \Pi_{AM}, af)$, with $\Pi_{AM} = \Omega \cup \Theta \cup \Delta \cup \Phi$, be a DeLP3E program, $\star \in$ **QAFO**, and Ψ be a revision objective function that can be computed in polynomial time. If we have that:*

1. *$|\{\lambda \mid \lambda \in \mathscr{W}_{EM} \text{ and } Pr(\lambda) > 0\}| \in O(poly(n))$, where n represents the size of the input;*
2. *$Pr(\lambda)$ can be computed in PTIME for any $\lambda \in \mathscr{W}_{EM}$; and*
3. *the PTW assumption holds,*

then deciding if $\Psi(\mathscr{I}, \mathscr{I} \star (f, af'), (f, af')) \leq k$ for some $k \in \mathbb{R}$, is NP-complete.

The construction used in the proof of Theorem 4.4 (cf. [11]) uses a very powerful objective function that essentially encodes the NP-hard problem and, furthermore, this objective function is not based on WPFs. We now provide an alternative result that proves NP-completeness under the same conditions, but assumes that the objective function is simply the sum of the probabilities assigned by the WPF to the set of ground atoms in the language associated with the AM.

Theorem 4.5 *Let $\mathscr{I} = (\Pi_{EM}, \Pi_{AM}, af)$, with $\Pi_{AM} = \Omega \cup \Theta \cup \Delta \cup \Phi$, be a DeLP3E program, $\star \in$ **QAFO**, and Ψ be a revision objective function that can be computed in polynomial time. If we have that:*

1. *$|\{\lambda \mid \lambda \in \mathscr{W}_{EM} \text{ and } Pr(\lambda) > 0\}| \in O(poly(n))$, where n represents the size of the input;*
2. *$Pr(\lambda)$ can be computed in PTIME for any $\lambda \in \mathscr{W}_{EM}$; and*
3. *the PTW assumption holds,*

then deciding if $\Psi(\mathscr{I}, \mathscr{I} \star (f, af'), (f, af')) \leq k$ for some $k \in \mathbb{R}$, is NP-complete even when Ψ is defined as $\sum_{a \in \mathbf{G}_{AM}} \Upsilon(a)$.

So, the Theorem 4.5 illustrates that the quantified revision problem is NP-hard when the EM and the number of EM worlds, and (hence) the computation of the WPF is not a source of complexity—even when the ROF used is a simple aggregate over WPFs of atoms. Further, as we can embed the Simple Max Cut problem, the

ROF—even a simple sum over WPFs—will not necessarily be monotonic, even when using a revision operator that satisfies the Inclusion postulate (where the set of worlds satisfying $af^*(y) \subseteq af'(y)$). This also shows NP-completeness when the belief revision operator performs modifications to Π_{AM} (by removing elements, as discussed in [10]) as setting $af^*(y) = \neg x$ can be viewed as an operation that is equivalent to removing it from Π_{AM}.

We also note that the related problem of consolidation or contraction by *falsum*, where we start with an inconsistent program and then must adjust the annotation function to make it consistent, can also be shown to be NP-complete: we fix the epistemic input to True, and change the rules of the form $set_1(v_i) \leftarrow query, \neg set_1(v_i) \leftarrow query$ to facts of the form $set_1(v_i), \neg set_1(v_i)$.

4.3.5   Warranting Formulas

We now focus on an algorithmic approach that can be used to compute approximate solutions and therefore address the computational intractability that we have seen in the results above.

In the following, given a dialectical forest $\mathscr{F}(L)$ and a node V corresponding to argument A, we will use the notation $label(V) = \bigwedge_{c \in A} af(c)$. For a given probabilistic argumentation framework, literal, and dialectical tree, Algorithm warrantFormula in Fig. 4.12 computes the formula describing the set of possible worlds that are warranting scenarios for the literal. Intuitively, this algorithm creates a formula for every dialectical tree in the forest associated with an argument—the algorithm iteratively builds a formula associated with the environmental conditions under which the argument in the root of the tree is undefeated. It then returns the disjunction of all such formulas in that forest. We refer to this disjunction as the *warranting formula* for the literal.

Algorithm warrantFormula($\mathscr{F}$)

1. For each tree $(V,E) \in \mathscr{F}$ with $(V,E) = \mathscr{T}^*_i(\langle \mathscr{A}, L \rangle)$ do
2.   For each $v \in V$ with $label(v) = \bigwedge_{f_j \in \mathscr{A}'} af(f_j)$ do
3.   While $|V| > 1$ do
4.   For each $v = \langle \mathscr{A}', L' \rangle \in \{v' \in V \mid children(v') \subseteq leaves(V)\}$ do
5. $label(v) := label(v) \wedge \neg \bigwedge_{v' \in children(v)} \neg label(v')$;
6.   End for;
7. $V := V \setminus leaves(V)$;
8.   End while;
9. $f_i := label\big(root(\mathscr{T}^*_i(\langle \mathscr{A}, L \rangle))\big)$;
10.   End for;
11. End for;
12. Return $\bigvee_i f_i$.

Fig. 4.12 An algorithm that takes a classical dialectical forest and computes a logical formula specifying the possible worlds under which a given literal is warranted

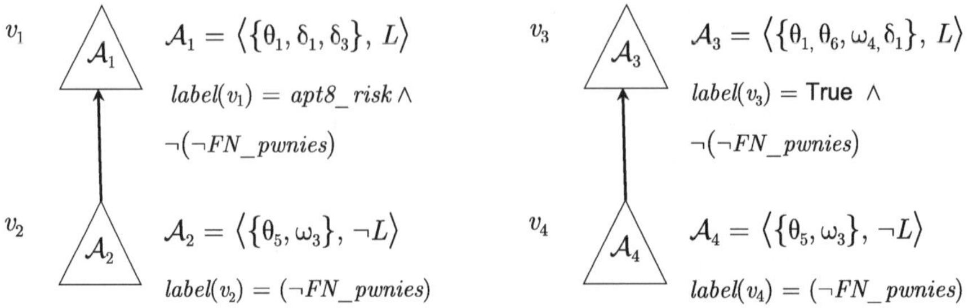

v_1 $\quad \mathcal{A}_1$ $\qquad \mathcal{A}_1 = \langle \{\theta_1, \delta_1, \delta_3\}, L \rangle$

$\qquad\qquad\qquad label(v_1) = apt8\_risk \wedge$

$\qquad\qquad\qquad \neg(\neg FN\_pwnies)$

v_2 $\quad \mathcal{A}_2$ $\qquad \mathcal{A}_2 = \langle \{\theta_5, \omega_3\}, \neg L \rangle$

$\qquad\qquad\qquad label(v_2) = (\neg FN\_pwnies)$

v_3 $\quad \mathcal{A}_3$ $\qquad \mathcal{A}_3 = \langle \{\theta_1, \theta_6, \omega_4, \delta_1\}, L \rangle$

$\qquad\qquad\qquad label(v_3) = \mathsf{True} \wedge$

$\qquad\qquad\qquad \neg(\neg FN\_pwnies)$

v_4 $\quad \mathcal{A}_4$ $\qquad \mathcal{A}_4 = \langle \{\theta_5, \omega_3\}, \neg L \rangle$

$\qquad\qquad\qquad label(v_4) = (\neg FN\_pwnies)$

Fig. 4.13 Dialectical forest for literal $L = exploit\_X$ composed of trees $\mathcal{T}_1$ (left) and $\mathcal{T}_2$ (right)

The following result states the correctness of the warrantFormula algorithm.

Proposition 4.6 *Given forest* $\mathscr{F}^*(L)$,

$$nec(L) = \Big\{ \lambda \in \mathscr{W}_{EM} \mid \lambda \models warrantFormula(\mathscr{F}^*(L)) \Big\}$$

$$poss(L) = \Big\{ \lambda \in \mathscr{W}_{EM} \mid \lambda \not\models warrantFormula(\mathscr{F}^*(\neg L)) \Big\}.$$

Even though warranting formulas are another way of solving the problem of computing probabilities exactly, our main motivation for developing it was to explore options for pursuing tractable algorithms, as discussed next.

The following is an example of the warranting formula approach in the setting of our running example.

Example 4.18 Consider the DeLP3E in our running example as shown in Fig. 4.11 with annotation function af_1. If we run Algorithm warrantFormula for literal *exploit_X*, we start with the dialectical forest shown in Fig. 4.13.

Suppose that the algorithm begins with tree $\mathcal{T}_1$ (on the left); the only leaf of this tree corresponds to vertex v_2 for argument $\mathcal{A}_2$, and its label remains the conjunction of all annotations of elements in the argument—$label(v_2) = \neg FN\_pwnies$. The algorithm then moves to the next node up, which is already the root, and updates the label by adding the conjunction with the negation of its child, which yields:

$$label(v_1) = apt8\_risk \wedge \neg(\neg FN\_pwnies) = apt8\_risk \wedge FN\_pwnies.$$

Processing tree $\mathcal{T}_2$ similarly yields:

$$label(v_3) = \mathsf{True} \wedge \neg(\neg FN\_pwnies) = FN\_pwnies.$$

Finally, the algorithm outputs the disjunction of these two formulas, which is simply *FN_pwnies*. ∎

4.3.6   Outlook: Towards Tractable Computations

By applying the warrantFormula algorithm to the dialectical forest for a given literal L, we can obtain the sets $nec(L)$ and $poss(L)$ with a running time proportional to the size of the forest and the annotation formulas—though the worst-time complexity has not been determined exactly, it is safe to conjecture that the worst case is intractable. However, the warranting formula approach opens the door to several possibilities for heuristics and approximate computations that either avoid exhaustively enumerating worlds in $\mathscr{W}_{EM}$ or working with full forests (or both). When combined with existing heuristics for classical argumentation (the AM) and probabilistic models (the EM), this provides us with a much more efficient way to compute warranting probability functions. Experimental evaluations for such hypotheses are currently underway.

The use of the warranting formula approach can have several impacts in the implementation of specific **QAFO** operators. First, warrant probability functions Υ in this setting can now be redefined to map elements in their domain to warranting formulas instead of probabilities as in their original formulation. Revision objective functions now have at their disposal formulas instead of raw numbers. This opens up the possibility for specific implementations to leverage optimizations such as applying SAT algorithms to decide whether $Pr_{\mathscr{I}_1}(L) \geq Pr_{\mathscr{I}_2}(L)$ (which can be decided via the SAT check $\Upsilon_{\mathscr{I}_1}(L) \Rightarrow \Upsilon_{\mathscr{I}_2}(L)$). Such an approach is clearly compatible with heuristic optimizations that may, for instance, sacrifice precision for greater tractability.

An alternative class of operators can thus be defined based on the same ideas as **QAFO** except that approximations are allowed instead of exact computations. There is much work to be done in this direction, which is outside the scope of the current book.

4.4   Conclusions and Future Work

In this chapter, we focused on characterizing belief revision operations over DeLP3E knowledge bases. In the first part, we presented two sets of postulates, both inspired by the postulates that were developed for non-prioritized revision of classical belief bases. The first set of postulates provides a coarse approach that assumes that revision operations only allow changes to the analytical model, while the second is a finer-grained approach based on modifications to the annotation function, yielding a class that called **AFO**. We then proceeded to study constructions of operators based on these postulates, and prove that they are equivalent to their characterizations by the respective postulates.

In the second part, we aimed to further explore the **AFO** class by considering operators that have the further requirement of "quantitative optimality"—this gave rise to the **QAFO** class of operators. Though this optimality criterion was kept as general as possible so that knowledge engineers can specify their preferences, we explored the computational complexity of the approach in general, arriving at a host of results that range from intractability for the general case to polynomial-time special cases. Finally, we presented an algorithm designed to compute the probability with which a literal is warranted via so-called warranting formulas, and provide some initial discussion regarding how this approach could be applied in the implementation of **QAFO** operators or approximations of them that trade theoretical guarantees for tractability in practice.

References

1. M. Capobianco, C. I. Chesñevar, and G. R. Simari. Argumentation and the dynamics of warranted beliefs in changing environments. *Journal on Autonomous Agents and Multiagent Systems*, 11:127–151, Sept. 2005.
2. L. A. Cecchi and G. R. Simari. El marcado de un árbol dialéctico en DeLP es PSPACE-completo. In *Proceedings of Congreso Argentino de Ciencias de la Computación (CACIC)*, 2011.
3. V. Chvátal. *Linear Programming*. W.H.Freeman, New York, 1983.
4. R. Fagin, J. Y. Halpern, and N. Megiddo. A logic for reasoning about probabilities. *Information and Computation*, 87(1/2):78–128, 1990.
5. M. A. Falappa, G. Kern-Isberner, M. Reis, and G. R. Simari. Prioritized and non-prioritized multiple change on belief bases. *Journal of Philosophical Logic*, 41(1):77–113, 2012.
6. A. J. García and G. R. Simari. Defeasible logic programming: An argumentative approach. *Theory and Practice of Logic Programming*, 4(1–2):95–138, 2004.
7. S. Hansson. Semi-revision. *Journal of Applied Non-Classical Logics*, 7(1–2):151–175, 1997.
8. N. J. Nilsson. Probabilistic logic. *Artificial Intelligence*, 28(1):71–87, 1986.
9. P. Shakarian, G. I. Simari, G. Moores, S. Parsons, and M. A. Falappa. An argumentation-based framework to address the attribution problem in cyber-warfare. In *Proceedings of the ASE International Conference on Cyber Security*, 2014.
10. P. Shakarian, G. I. Simari, G. Moores, D. Paulo, S. Parsons, M. A. Falappa, and A. Aleali. Belief revision in structured probabilistic argumentation: Model and application to cyber security. *Annals of Mathematics and Artificial Intelligence*, 78(3–4):259–301, 2016.
11. G. I. Simari, P. Shakarian, and M. A. Falappa. A quantitative approach to belief revision in structured probabilistic argumentation. *Annals of Mathematics and Artificial Intelligence*, 76(3–4):375–408, 2016.
12. S. Toda. On the computational power of PP and ⊕P. In *Proc. of FOCS*, pages 514–519, 1989.

Chapter 5
Applying Argumentation Models for Cyber Attribution

5.1 Introduction

As we have shown and argued in previous chapters, cyber attribution is one of the central technical and policy challenges in cybersecurity—the main reasons for this is that oftentimes the evidence collected from multiple sources provides a contradictory viewpoint, and this gets worse in cases of deception where either an attacker plants false evidence or the evidence points to multiple actors. In Chap. 3 we proposed DeLP3E to address this issue using formal logic-based tools; in this chapter, we discuss:

- how a model for cyber attribution can be designed and implemented in the DeLP3E framework;
- experiments demonstrating that using argumentation-based tools can significantly reduce the number of potential culprits that need to be considered in the analysis of a cyberattack; and
- experiments showing that the reduced set of culprits, used in conjunction with classification, leads to improved cyber attribution decisions.

The DeLP3E models used in this chapter are a subset of DeLP3E since they don't involve probabilistic reasoning; such models are thus equivalent to classical (Pre)DeLP models.

Preliminaries Before describing our models in detail, we recall some notation introduced in previous chapters. Variables and constant symbols represent items such as the exploits/payloads used for the attack, and the actors conducting the cyberattack (in this case, the teams in the CTF competition). We denote the set of all variable symbols with **V** and the set of all constants with **C**. For our model we require two subsets of **C**: $\mathbf{C}_{act}$, denoting the actors capable of conducting the

© The Author(s) 2018
E. Nunes et al., *Artificial Intelligence Tools for Cyber Attribution*, SpringerBriefs in Computer Science, https://doi.org/10.1007/978-3-319-73788-1_5

Table 5.1 Example predicates and explanation

Predicate	Explanation
attack(*exploit*$_1$, *bluelotus*)	*exploit*$_1$ was targeted towards the team Blue Lotus
replay_attack($\mathcal{E}$, *Y*)	Exploit $\mathcal{E}$ was replayed by team *Y*
deception(*exploit*$_1$, *apt8*)	Team *apt8* used *exploit*$_1$ for deception
time_diff(*I*, *Y*)	Team *Y* was deceptive within the given time interval *I*
culprit(*exploit*$_1$, *apt8*)	Team *apt8* is the likely culprit for the attack (using *exploit*$_1$ on the target team)

cyberoperation, and $\mathbf{C}_{ops}$, denoting the set of unique exploits used. We use symbols in all capital letters to denote variables. In the running example, we use a subset of our DEFCON CTF dataset.

Example 5.1 The following are examples of actors and cyberoperations appearing in the CTF data:

$$\mathbf{C}_{act} = \{bluelotus, robotmafia, apt8\},$$

$$\mathbf{C}_{ops} = \{exploit_1, exploit_2, \ldots, exploit_n\}.$$

∎

The language also contains a set of predicate symbols that have constants or variables as arguments, and denote events that can be either *true* or *false*. We denote the set of predicates with $\mathbf{P}_{AM}$; examples of predicates are shown in Table 5.1. For instance, *culprit*(*exploit*$_1$, *apt8*) will either be true or false, and denotes the event where *apt8* used *exploit*$_1$ to conduct a cyberoperation.

A ground atom is composed by a predicate symbol and a tuple of constants, one for each argument. The set of all ground atoms is denoted as $\mathbf{G}_{AM}$. A ground literal L is a ground atom or a negated ground atom; hence, ground literals have no variables. An example of a ground atom for our running example is *attack*(*exploit*$_1$, *bluelotus*). We denote a subset of $\mathbf{G}_{AM}$ with $\mathbf{G}'_{AM}$.

Finally, recall that DeLP3E programs are comprised of an analytical model (AM), an environmental model (EM), and an annotation function relating elements from the former with elements from the latter; however, only the AM is of interest in the models developed in this chapter. We thus adopt the usual notation for (Pre)DeLP programs, denoting the knowledge base with $\Pi = (\Theta, \Omega, \Phi, \Delta)$, where Θ is the set of facts, Ω is the set of strict rules, Φ is the set of presumptions, and Δ is the set of defeasible rules. Examples of these constructs are provided with respect to the CTF dataset in Fig. 5.1. For instance, θ_1 indicates the fact that *exploit*$_1$ was used to target the team *Blue Lotus*, and θ_5 indicates that team *pwnies* is the most frequent user of *exploit*$_1$. For the strict rules, ω_1 says that for a given *exploit*$_1$ the attacker is *pwnies* if it was the most frequent attacker and the attack *exploit*$_1$ was replayed. Defeasible rules can be read similarly; δ_2 indicates that *exploit*$_1$ was used in a deceptive attack by APT8 if it was replayed and the first attacker was not

Θ : $\theta_1 =$ attack($exploit_1, bluelotus$)
$\theta_2 =$ first_attack($exploit_1, robotmafia$)
$\theta_3 =$ last_attack($exploit_1, apt8$))
$\theta_4 =$ time_diff($interval, robotmafia$)
$\theta_5 =$ most_frequent($exploit_1, pwnies$)

Ω : $\omega_1 =$ culprit($exploit_1, pwnies$) $\leftarrow$
            most_frequent($exploit_1, pwnies$),
            replay_attack($exploit_1$)
$\omega_2 = \neg$ culprit($exploit_1, robotMafia$) $\leftarrow$
            last_attack($exploit_1, apt8$),
            replay_attack($exploit_1$)

Δ : $\delta_1 =$ replay_attack($exploit_1$) $\prec$
            attack($exploit_1, bluelotus$),
            last_attack($exploit_1, apt8$)
$\delta_2 =$ deception($exploit_1, apt8$) $\prec$
            replay_attack($exploit_1$),
            first_attack($exploit_1, robotmafia$)
$\delta_3 =$ culprit($exploit_1, apt8$) $\prec$
            deception($exploit_1, apt8$),
            replay_attack($exploit_1$)
$\delta_4 = \neg$culprit($exploit_1, apt8$) $\prec$
            time_diff($interval, robotmafia$)

Fig. 5.1 A ground argumentation framework

$\langle \mathscr{A}_1,$ replay_attack($exploit_1$) $\rangle$	$\mathscr{A}_1 = \{\delta_1, \theta_1, \theta_3\}$
$\langle \mathscr{A}_2,$ deception($exploit_1, apt8$) $\rangle$	$\mathscr{A}_2 = \{\delta_1, \delta_2, \theta_2\}$
$\langle \mathscr{A}_3,$ culprit($exploit_1, apt8$)$\rangle$	$\mathscr{A}_3 = \{\delta_1, \delta_2, \delta_3\}$
$\langle \mathscr{A}_4, \neg$culprit($exploit_1, apt8$)$\rangle$	$\mathscr{A}_4 = \{\delta_1, \delta_4, \theta_3\}$

Fig. 5.2 Example ground arguments from Fig. 5.1

APT8. By replacing the constants with variables in the predicates we can derive a non-ground argumentation framework.

Figure 5.2 shows example arguments based on the KB from Fig. 5.1; here, $\langle \mathscr{A}_1,$ replay_attack($exploit_1$)$\rangle$ is a subargument of $\langle \mathscr{A}_2,$ deception($exploit_1, apt8$)$\rangle$ and $\langle \mathscr{A}_3,$ culprit($exploit_1, apt8$)$\rangle$. Furthermore, we can see that $\mathscr{A}_4$ attacks $\mathscr{A}_3$.

5.2 Baseline Argumentation Model (BM)

In Chap. 2 we discussed how machine learning techniques can be leveraged to identify attackers; let us recall briefly the setup, since the experiments reported on here follow the same structure. The dataset was divided according to the target team, yielding 20 subsets, and all the attacks were then sorted according to time. The first 90% of the attacks were reserved for training, and the remaining 10% for testing. The byte and instruction histograms were used as features to train and test

$\omega_1 = $ culprit$(\mathcal{E}, Y) \leftarrow $ last_attack$(\mathcal{E}, Y)$, replay_attack$(\mathcal{E})$.

$\delta_1 = $ replay_attack$(\mathcal{E}) \prec $ attack$(\mathcal{E}, X)$, last_attack$(\mathcal{E}, Y)$.

Fig. 5.3 Defeasible and strict rule for non-deceptive attack

the models. The approaches based on random forest classifiers [1, 2] performed the best, with an average accuracy of 0.37; most of the misclassified samples corresponded to deceptive attacks and their duplicates.

When using machine learning approaches it is difficult to map the reasons why a particular attacker was predicted, especially in cases of deception where multiple attackers were associated with the same attack. Knowing the arguments that supported a particular decision would greatly aid the analyst in making better decisions dealing with uncertainty. To address this issue we now describe how we can form arguments/rules based on the latent variables computed from the training data, given an attack for attribution.

We use the following notation: let $\mathcal{E}$ be the test attack under consideration aimed at target team X, Y represent all the possible attacking teams, and $\mathcal{D}$ be the set of all deceptive teams (those using the same payload to target the same team) if the given attack is deceptive in the training set. For non-deceptive attacks, $\mathcal{D}$ will be empty. We note that facts cannot have variables, only constants (however, to compress the program for presentation purposes, we use *meta-variables* in facts). To begin, we define the facts:

$$\theta_1 = \text{attack } (\mathcal{E}, X), \quad \theta_2 = \text{first\_attack } (\mathcal{E}, Y), \quad \theta_3 = \text{last\_attack } (\mathcal{E}, Y);$$

θ_1 states that attack $\mathcal{E}$ was used to target team X, θ_2 states that team Y was the first team to use the attack $\mathcal{E}$ in the training data, and similarly θ_3 states that team Y was the last team to use the attack $\mathcal{E}$ in the training data. The first and last attacking team may or may not be the same. We study the following three cases:

Case 1: Non-Deceptive Attacks In non-deceptive attacks, only one team uses the payload to target other teams in the training data. It is easy to predict the attacker for these cases, since the search space only has one team. To model this situation, we define a set of defeasible and strict rules.

In Fig. 5.3, defeasible rule δ_1 checks whether the attack was replayed in the training data. Since it is a non-deceptive attack, it can only be replayed by the same team. The strict rule ω_1 then puts forth an argument for the attacker (culprit) if the defeasible rule holds and there is no contradiction for it.

Case 2: Deceptive Attacks These attacks form the majority of the misclassified samples in Chap. 2. The set $\mathcal{D}$ is not empty for this case; let $\mathcal{D}_i$ denote the deceptive teams in $\mathcal{D}$. We also compute the most frequent attacker from the training data given a deceptive attack. Let the most frequent deceptive attacker be denoted as F. The DeLP components that model this case are shown in Fig. 5.4; fact θ_1 indicates

$\theta_1 = \text{decep}(\mathcal{E}, X), \theta_2 = \text{frequent}(\mathcal{E}, F)$

$\omega_1 = \neg\text{culprit}(\mathcal{E}, Y) \leftarrow \text{first\_attack}(\mathcal{E}, Y), \text{decep}(\mathcal{E}, X)$
$\omega_2 = \text{culprit}(\mathcal{E}, F) \leftarrow \text{frequent}(\mathcal{E}, F), \text{deception}(\mathcal{E}, \mathcal{D}_i)$

$\delta_1 = \text{replay\_attack}(\mathcal{E}) \prec \text{attack}(\mathcal{E}, X), \text{last\_attack}(\mathcal{E}, Y)$
$\delta_2 = \text{deception}(\mathcal{E}, \mathcal{D}_i) \prec \text{replay\_attack}(\mathcal{E}),$
$\qquad\qquad\qquad \text{first\_attack}(\mathcal{E}, Y)$
$\delta_3 = \text{culprit}(\mathcal{E}, \mathcal{D}_i) \prec \text{deception}(\mathcal{E}, \mathcal{D}_i), \text{first\_attack}(\mathcal{E}, Y)$

Fig. 5.4 Facts and rules for deceptive attacks

if the attack $\mathcal{E}$ was deceptive towards the team X and θ_2 indicates the most frequent attacker team F from the training set. The strict rule ω_1 indicates that in case of deception the first team to attack (Y) is not the attacker, ω_2 states that the attacker should be F if the attack is deceptive and F was the most frequent deceptive attacker. For the defeasible rules, δ_1 deals with the case in which the attack $\mathcal{E}$ was replayed, δ_2 deals with the case of deceptive teams from the set $\mathcal{D}$, δ_3 indicates that all the deceptive teams are likely to be the attackers in the absence of any contradictory information. and δ_4 states that the attacker should be F if the attack is deceptive and F was the most frequent attacker.

Case 3: Previously Unseen Attacks The most difficult attacks to attribute in the dataset are the unseen ones, i.e. attacks first encountered in the test set and thus did not occur in the training set. To build constructs for this kind of attack we first compute the k nearest neighbors from the training set according to a simple Euclidean distance between the byte and instruction histograms of the two attacks. In this case we choose $k = 3$. For each of the matching attacks from the training data we check if the attack is deceptive or non-deceptive. If non-deceptive, we follow the procedure for Case 1, otherwise we follow the procedure for Case 2. Since we replace one unseen attack with three seen attacks, the search space for the attacker increases for unseen attacks.

Attacker Time Analysis The CTF data provides us with timestamps for the attacks in the competition. We can use this information to come up with rules for/against an argument for a team being the attacker. We compute the average time for a team to replay its own attack given that it was the first one to deploy the attack (see Fig. 5.5). It can be observed that teams like *More Smoked Leet Chicken* (T-13) and *Wowhacker-bios* (T-8) are very quick to replay their own attacks as compared to other teams. Figure 5.5 also shows the average time for a team to perform a deceptive attack. Teams like *The European* (T-7) and *Blue Lotus* (T-10) are quick to commit deception, while others take more time.

We use this time information to narrow down our search space for possible attackers. In particular, for a deceptive test sample, we compute the time difference between the test sample and the training sample that last used the same payload. We denote this time difference as $\triangle t$, and include it as a fact θ_1. We then divide the

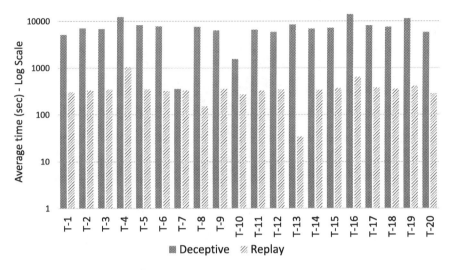

Fig. 5.5 Average time for team to perform a deceptive attack and replay its own attack (Log-scale)

$\Theta : \theta_1 = \text{timedifference} (\mathscr{E}, X)$

For $Y \notin$ interval:
$\Delta : \delta_1 = \neg\text{culprit}(\mathscr{E}, Y) \prec \text{timedifference} (\mathscr{E}, X).$

Fig. 5.6 Time facts and rules. Interval indicates a small portion of the entire deceptive time (for instance less than 2000 s, greater than 8000 s and so on)

deceptive times from Fig. 5.5 into appropriate intervals; each team is assigned to one of those time intervals. We then check which time interval Δt belongs to and define a defeasible rule δ_1 that makes a case for all teams not belonging to the interval to not be the culprits, as shown in Fig. 5.6.

We now provide a summary of the experimental results—the constructs for all test samples based on the cases discussed in the previous section are computed, and these arguments are used as input to the DeLP engine. For each test sample, the DeLP system is queried to find all possible attackers (culprits) based on the arguments provided. If there is no way to decide between contradicting arguments, these are blocked and thus return no answers. Initially, the search space for each test sample is 19 teams (all except the one being attacked).

After running the queries to return the set of possible culprits, the average search space across all target teams is 5.85 teams. This is a significant reduction in search space across all target teams; to gauge how much the reduced search space can aid an analyst in predicting the actual culprit, a metric is computed that checks if the reduced search space contains the ground truth (actual culprit). For all the target teams, the ground truth is present on average in almost 66% of the samples with reduced search space. For some teams like *More Smoked Leet Chicken* (T-13) and *Raon_ASRT (whois)* (T-17) the average reduced search space is as low as 1.82 and 2.9 teams, with high ground truth fractions of 0.69 and 0.63, respectively.

Predictive analysis is then performed on the reduced search space. The experimental setup is similar to the one described earlier; the only difference this time is instead of having a 19 team search space as in Chap. 2, the machine learning approach is allowed to make a prediction from the reduced search space only; a random forest is used for learning, since it was the one with the best performance for this CTF data in our previous experiments.

We report the following average accuracies across 20 target teams; the accuracy achieved after running random forest without applying the argumentation-based techniques, as reported in Chap. 2, is 0.37. This was the best performing approach using standard machine learning techniques. The baseline model achieves an average accuracy of 0.5, which is already significantly better. We will now explore several ways in which this baseline argumentation model can be improved.

5.3   Extended Baseline Model I (EB1)

Previously unseen attacks make up almost 20% of the test samples for each target team. On analyzing the misclassification from the baseline argumentation model, we observe that the majority of the previously unseen attacks get misclassified (more than 80%). The misclassifications can be attributed to two reasons: (i) the reduced search space is not able to capture the ground truth for unseen attacks, leading the learning model to a wrong prediction; and (ii) we represent each unseen attack by the three most similar attacks in the training data; this leads to an increase in the search space, which translates to more choices for the learning model.

We address these issues by proposing two sets of defeasible rules. First, for each target team we compute from the training set the top three teams that come up with the most unique exploits, as these teams are more likely to launch an unseen attack in the test set. The intuition behind this rule is the fact that not all teams write their own exploits, most teams just capture a successful exploit launched by other teams and repackage it and use it as their own (deception). The second set of rules is proposed to avoid addition of less similar teams to the reduced search space. In the baseline model we use 3-nearest neighbors to represent an unseen attack. In this extended version we consider only the nearest neighbors that are less than a particular threshold value T, which is decided for each target team separately. So, each attack will be represented by $k \leq 3$ teams depending upon the threshold requirement. In addition to the baseline model rules, we propose the following rules for deceptive attacks. Let $\mathcal{U}$ denote the set of teams with the three highest numbers of unique attacks in the training data. Also, let $\mathcal{N}$ denote the set of three most similar culprits for the given unseen attack.

The extended model is shown in Fig. 5.7; the fact θ_1 indicates the teams present in $\mathcal{N}$ and whose similarity is less than a particular threshold T, and θ_2 indicates if the team u_i was one of most unique attackers from set $\mathcal{U}$. For the defeasible

$$
\begin{array}{l}
\qquad\qquad \text{For } (n_i \in \mathcal{N} \text{ and } sim < T): \\
\Theta : \theta_1 = \mathsf{threshold}(\mathscr{E}, T) \\
\qquad\qquad \text{For } u_i \text{ in } \mathcal{U}: \\
\qquad\quad \theta_2 = \mathsf{unique}(\mathscr{E}, u_i) \\
\hline
\Delta : \delta_1 = \mathsf{culprit}(\mathscr{E}, u_i) \prec \mathsf{threshold}(\mathscr{E}, T) \\
\qquad\qquad \text{For } u_i \in \mathcal{U}: \\
\qquad\quad \delta_2 = \mathsf{culprit}(\mathscr{E}, u_i) \prec \mathsf{unique}(\mathscr{E}, u_i)
\end{array}
$$

Fig. 5.7 Rules for previously unseen attacks

rules, δ_1 makes use of the fact θ_1 stating that the teams in $\mathcal{N}$ that satisfy the threshold condition are likely to be the culprits, and δ_2 indicates that if u_i is a unique attacker then it can be the culprit unless contradictory information is available. $\mathcal{U}$ is independent of the test samples and will be the same for all previously unseen attacks given a target team.

On the contrary, for each of the similar payloads (three or fewer) computed from the training data we check if the attack is deceptive or non-deceptive. If non-deceptive, we follow the procedure for Case 1, otherwise we follow the procedure for Case 2 stated in the baseline argumentation model.

Experimental Results We evaluate EB1 using an experimental setup similar to the one for the baseline argumentation model. We report the average reduced search space and prediction accuracy for both EB1 and baseline model to provide a comparison. EB1 performs better than the baseline with an average accuracy of 0.53 vs. 0.50, and significantly better than the machine learning model without argumentation (with an average accuracy of 0.37). The improvement in performance is due to the larger fraction of reduced search spaces with ground truth present in them. Also, the search space reduced from on average 6.07 teams to 5.025 (less teams to consider). The results are reported in Table 5.2, along with a comparison with the second extended baseline argumentation model (EB2), which is described next.

5.4   Extended Baseline Model II (EB2)

Another source of misclassification in the baseline argumentation model is the presence of previously unseen deceptive teams and their duplicates. These refer to teams that did not use the exploit in the training set but started using it in the test set. It is difficult for a machine learning approach to predict such a team as being the culprit if it has not encountered it using the exploit in the training set. In our dataset these attacks comprise 15% of the total, and up to 20% for some teams.

Table 5.2 Summary of results

Team	ML [3]	BM	EB1	EB2
T-1	0.45	0.51	0.52	**0.60**
T-2	0.22	**0.45**	0.38	0.43
T-3	0.30	0.40	0.47	**0.66**
T-4	0.26	0.44	0.42	**0.44**
T-5	0.26	0.45	0.45	**0.56**
T-6	0.5	0.49	0.55	**0.7**
T-7	0.45	0.53	0.56	**0.66**
T-8	0.42	0.61	0.58	**0.74**
T-9	0.41	0.50	0.53	**0.76**
T-10	0.30	0.42	**0.41**	**0.41**
T-11	0.37	0.44	0.5	**0.73**
T-12	0.24	0.43	0.36	**0.52**
T-13	0.35	0.63	0.64	**0.75**
T-14	0.42	0.52	0.53	**0.67**
T-15	0.30	0.38	0.55	**0.64**
T-16	0.43	0.48	0.55	**0.65**
T-17	0.42	0.58	0.58	**0.68**
T-18	0.48	0.50	0.52	**0.65**
T-19	0.41	0.51	0.56	**0.68**
T-20	0.48	0.51	0.64	**0.71**

The bold values in the table indicate the best performing model for the team

$$\Theta : \theta_1 = \text{timedifference}\,(\mathscr{E}, X)$$

For $Y \in$ interval:
$$\Delta : \delta_1 = \text{culprit}(\mathscr{E}, Y) \prec \text{timedifference}\,(\mathscr{E}, X).$$

Fig. 5.8 Time facts and rules. Interval indicates a small portion of the entire deceptive time (for instance, less than 2000 s, greater than 8000 s, and so on)

In order to address this issue we propose an extension of EB1, where we group together teams that have similar deceptive behavior based on the time information available to us from the training set; for instance teams that are deceptive within a certain interval of time (e.g., less than 2000 s) after the first attack has been played are grouped together. For a given test attack we compute the time difference between the test attack and the last time the attack was used in the training set. We then assign this time difference to a specific group based on which interval the time difference falls in. In order to fine tune the time intervals, instead of using the average deceptive times averaged across all target teams (as used in the baseline model), we compute and use deceptive times for each target team separately. We model the time rules as stated in Fig. 5.8; fact θ_1 states the time difference between the test sample and the last training sample to use that attack, defeasible rule δ_1 on the other hand states that teams belonging to that interval (in which the time difference lies) are likely to be the culprits unless a contradiction is present. It is clear that this rule will increase the search space for the test sample, as additional teams are now being added as likely culprits. We observe that for EB2 the search space is increased by an average of almost 2.5 teams per test sample from EB1; at the same time the presence of ground truth in the reduced search space increased to 0.78, which is a significant improvement over 0.68.

Experimental Results We evaluate EB2 using an experimental setup similar to the one discussed in the baseline argumentation model. We report the prediction accuracies for each of the proposed baseline argumentation models for each of the target teams and compare it with the previous accuracy reported in Chap. 2, denoted as ML. In Table 5.2, the second extended baseline model (EB2) performs the best with an average prediction accuracy of 62%, as compared to other proposed methods. The addition of teams based on time rules not only benefits detection of unseen deceptive teams but it also helps in predicting attackers for unseen attacks. The major reason for the jump in performance is that for most unseen deceptive team samples, the time rules proposed in the baseline model block all deceptive teams from being the culprit, leading to an empty set of culprits. The new set of rules proposed in EB2 adds similar-behaving teams to this set based on time information; the learning algorithm can then predict the right one from this set.

5.5 Conclusions

In this chapter we demonstrated how our argumentation-based framework (DeLP3E) can be leveraged to improve cyber attribution decisions by building models based on CTF data that afford a reduction of the set of potential culprits and thus greater accuracy when using a classifier for cyber attribution. These first steps were taken using DeLP3E models with an empty EM (that is, without probabilistic information); current and future work involves extending these models to leverage uncertainty.

In Chap. 6 we discuss designing our own CTF event in order to better mimic real-world scenarios. In particular, it will encourage deceptive behavior among the participants, and we are also enhancing our instrumentation of the CTF in order to allow for additional data collection (host data is of particular interest). This richer data will also help build models that take uncertainty into account.

References

1. L. Breiman. Bagging predictors. *Machine learning*, 24(2):123–140, 1996.
2. L. Breiman. Random forests. *Machine learning*, 45(1):5–32, 2001.
3. E. Nunes, N. Kulkarni, P. Shakarian, A. Ruef, and J. Little. Cyber-deception and attribution in capture-the-flag exercises. In *Proceedings of the IEEE/ACM International Conference on Advances in Social Networks Analysis and Mining (ASONAM)*, pages 962–965, 2015.

Chapter 6
Enhanced Data Collection for Cyber Attribution

6.1 Introduction

In the aftermath of a cyberattack or breach, a natural question to ask after discovery is "who did it?". This question is important in a variety of contexts: to determine the proportionate defender response, to guide law enforcement investigations, and to perform damage assessment and risk exposure of any data lost. However, how does an analyst assess an attribution decision? To guide the creation of our attribution processes and systems, we require data to train on where we can have ground truth. To help guide the creation of the attribution systems that we have described in previous chapters by creating data usable for attribution research with believable ground truth, we propose using computer security games similar to the Capture-the-Flag (CTF) setting described in Chap. 2, but with more data available. Such a framework must not only encourage contestants to obtain access to target systems, but must also encourage them to employ stealth and deception while conducting operations.

We created a game framework where contestants are motivated to deceive other contestants in a computer security setting. This game framework challenges contestants to attack containerized systems while leaving as little of a trace as possible, and to analyze the traces left by other contestants attempting to attribute those traces to specific contestants. We implemented this framework as a Linux system using Docker containers and the Linux container framework to isolate users from each other and create a game environment hosted on a single system. The goal of this game framework is to produce data useful to cyber attribution research. We make our platform available as open-source software. It can be downloaded from [3].

© The Author(s) 2018
E. Nunes et al., *Artificial Intelligence Tools for Cyber Attribution*, SpringerBriefs in Computer Science, https://doi.org/10.1007/978-3-319-73788-1_6

6.2   Goals and Design

As described in Chap. 2, the goal of a capture-the-flag event is to present a game environment that preserves the essence of the computer security ecosystem. Teams are charged with simultaneously identifying vulnerabilities in their own systems and patching them as well as identifying vulnerabilities in the other competitors systems and exploiting them. Teams are unaware of the exact nature and location of the flaws they have to find. The scoring algorithm strongly penalizes the lack of availability of a teams services, even if those services are vulnerable. Teams must walk a tightrope where they have to favor availability over security, monitor their potentially vulnerable systems closely to identify attacks from other teams, and exploit other teams without making those teams aware of their vulnerability.

DEFCON CTF [1] rewards contestants for keeping their systems available and exploiting other teams. We want to add an additional dimension to the game: we would like contestants to actively attempt to deceive the teams they are attacking into believing that a different team was the source of the attack. In the existing CTF game concept there is little reason to do this. By motivating the contestants to employ deception, the data we gather will be more relevant to studying deception in attribution while retaining ground truth. As the "game masters", we can maintain visibility of the true facts of the game, and we can contrast contestant performance with the performance of algorithms developed for the purpose of countering deception.

6.2.1   Changing Contestant Behavior

In a game, contestants are presented with a game environment and a winning objective. The game environment gives the contestants a way to make incremental progress towards the winning objective, usually by acquiring points for completing some action. If the game designer wants the contestants to do specific actions, they should reward those actions with points. The designer should also take care to balance the scoring system to not create perverse incentives or to create incentives that the designer explicitly does not want.

In traditional attack/defend CTFs like DEFCON CTF, the organizers want contestants to reverse engineer programs, find vulnerabilities, write exploits, and use those exploits against other teams. They also want the other teams to present a challenging target for the use of the exploits. To motivate these activities, the CTF scoring system awards points to a team if that team is able to capture another teams "flag," almost always represented as a token stored in a file or in memory.

We want to borrow this motivation to reward contestants for finding and exploiting vulnerabilities, however we also want contestants to try and cover their tracks or otherwise be deceptive about their origins.

6.2.2 Game Rules

Our game is split into two distinct phases (see Fig. 6.1). In the first phase, contestants are given three programs and asked to identify a vulnerability in each program. The contestants demonstrate that they have found the vulnerability by exploiting a running instance of the program and presenting a key to the scoring infrastructure. While they do this, a trace of the traffic they send to the running programs is collected, as well as host-level interactions that occur in the context of the vulnerable running program. Because each instance of each running program is allocated uniquely per team, the infrastructure is able to gather ground truth that definitively maps the activities of an attacking team to a system under attack.

During the second phase, each contestant is asked to make three attribution decisions. For each decision the infrastructure chooses three successful attacks. The infrastructure knows when an attack was successful as the infrastructure knows which key was submitted for which vulnerable program instance. To create an attribution question for contestants, the infrastructure chooses three successful attacks and presents the network traffic associated with those attacks. For two of the questions, the system reveals which team produced the network traffic. The choice of teams included in each question is not entirely random. The goal is to present the contestant with two known matches and see if they can infer from the known matches which team is matched with the unidentified traffic.

Fig. 6.1 Flow of game play. In Phase 1, players attack network services to capture flags, while their traffic is recorded by the game world. In Phase 2, the recordings are used to construct questions for contestants to answer about which team produced which packet capture while attacking a program

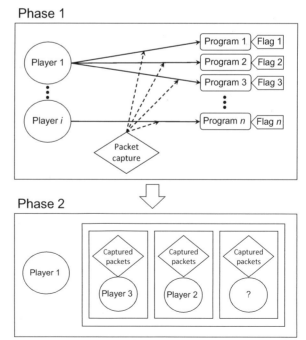

Each contestant has an overall score: a contestant gains ten points for each of the three vulnerable programs they exploit during the first phase; during the second phase, a contestant gains ten points for each attribution question in which they are not correctly identified, and loses ten points for each attribution question in which they are correctly identified. Finally, they also gain five points for each correct attribution decision they make, and lose no points for getting an attribution question incorrect.

6.2.3 Infrastructure Design

The infrastructure is designed to allow two goals: the contestants should be able to interact with "real" systems and hack them, while simultaneously the contestants should not be able to break the rules of the hacking competition itself by adjusting their score or gaining too much visibility into the activities in the game. Scalability is also desirable: hosting the system on fewer resources makes it more economical to run more experiments, and run them for longer periods of time.

The infrastructure uses a combination of Docker and Linux containers (lxc) managed through the *firejail* utility (see Fig. 6.2).[1] Each contestant is given a unique username and password that they use to access the system; these credentials authenticate them via PAM, however the contestant user's shell is set to firejail. The firejail utility, in turn, is configured to restrict the file system, process, and network resources that a contestant user may access. This is done to keep contestants separated from each other.

Each contestant user is statically matched to three Docker containers, each running a different, vulnerable program. Our vulnerable programs were curated from the Cyber Grand Challenge (CGC) Challenge Binary (CB) corpus [2]. There are more than 100 vulnerable programs available in this corpus, so different problems could be rotated in and out over time.

Each vulnerable binary is also assigned a unique flag. The flag is placed in a file alongside the vulnerable program within the Docker container. The scoring infrastructure recognizes and awards points for the compromise of a particular flag. This is used during the first phase of the contest to reward points for attacking services.

In addition to recording the traffic between users firejail sessions and vulnerable binaries, the infrastructure also uses the auditd infrastructure from Linux to record system calls and parameters throughout the system. This is useful because it adds an additional level of information to the contest, where that information is also available in a real world setting. This allows attribution researchers to consider the behavior of attackers once they have compromised a system, not just their behavior while attempting to compromise the host by exploiting it over the network.

---

[1] https://firejail.wordpress.com/.

Fig. 6.2 Contest
infrastructure design. Each
user is isolated both in the
network and process
visibility. Each user may only
connect to the challenges
assigned to them and, by
extension, only the flags that
have been allocated to them

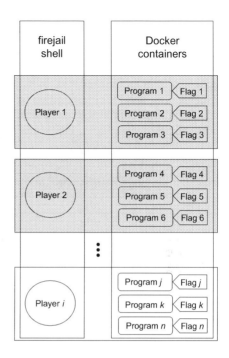

6.2.4 *Motivating Attribution and Deception*

There are a few possible choices for scoring attribution decisions. During the
attribution phase, there are two contestants playing against each other, rather than
one contestant as in the first phase. This is a trade-off in the design that allows for
asynchronous data collection while preserving the head to head nature of deception
and attribution. Consider the alternatives. In a traditional attack and defense CTF,
the contestants are all online at the same time and contesting the same digital
space. The interaction is much richer but the barrier to entry is much higher and
the organizational load is also higher. We strike a balance where contestants don't
need to be online all at the same time, but there is still the possibility for deception.

This is also our effort at making attribution a first class element of gameplay. In
other CTFs, attribution is a secondary concern to a team. When a team is scored
against, that team isn't given a motivation to try and attribute that action to a
particular team. They might be motivated to understand the attack, if the attack
is one they have not seen before, because they would like to not be scored against
again. It would be nice to give contestants a more natural motivation for attribution,
however that could come at the cost of a more expensive contest.

6.2.5   Validity of Data

To make the resulting data more suitable for attribution research, the produced data must match to actual intrusions. The type of data produced by this contest matches with data that would be produced by network defenders tracing their own networks. Network defenders can also trace their own hosts using the same auditd infrastructure that the game infrastructure uses.

An important issue to address is: does the behavior of the contestants match the behavior of attackers in the real world? This is partly a question of contestant recruitment and partly a question of incentives. We have worked to try to make the incentive structure match the real world: contestants only receive points when they hack into a system, but they lose points if someone is able to identify them as a result of their hacking. This matches the incentive structure in a criminal setting on the Internet: a computer criminal only profits if he attempts to hack into a system, but if he/she can be identified and prosecuted, then he/she clearly does not profit.

Contestants that compete in hacking competitions can be a fair proxy for attackers on the Internet. Like the Internet, there is a broad spectrum. Some contestants are students or learners of low skill, while others work professionally and view competing in contests as part of their professional identity. As long as the incentive structures are set up to get contestants to practice deception, the deception behavior of contestants should have real world validity.

6.3   Conclusion

In this chapter, we presented the framework, the design and implementation of a game framework to collect information that can be used in attribution research. The framework is made available publicly [3].

References

1. C. Cowan, S. Arnold, S. Beattie, C. Wright, and J. Viega. Defcon capture the flag: Defending vulnerable code from intense attack. In *DARPA Information Survivability Conference and Exposition, 2003. Proceedings*, volume 1, pages 120–129. IEEE, 2003.
2. DARPA. Cyber grand challenge, 2016. http://archive.darpa.mil/cybergrandchallenge/.
3. A. Ruef, E. Nunes, P. Shakarian, and G. I. Simari. Cyber attribution game framework. 2017. Available at https://github.com/trailofbits/attribution-vm.

Chapter 7
Conclusion

There are many challenges in the area of cyber attribution. It is easy and useful for an actor to perform deception, hindering the decision making ability of standard machine learning models to identify the actor as demonstrated in Chap. 2. Structured argumentation-based frameworks like DeLP can help alleviate deception to some extent by providing arguments for the selection of a particular actor/actors responsible for the attack based on the evidence. In Chap. 5, we provided results showing how such models afford significant performance improvements over approaches based solely on machine learning techniques.

An important challenge in cyber attribution is to train and evaluate the proposed models. This book presents a framework to collect data from hacking competitions, i.e. capture-the-flag events. The framework encourages and monitors competitors as they adopt deceptive behavior. In addition to just the network traffic, the framework is also capable of capturing host data. Other practical challenges include making attribution decisions in real time, and scaling the proposed models to larger datasets. Though challenging, we believe that these issues will be resolved as the research progresses.

We may be entering a golden age of threat intelligence. Modern security operations' practices and frameworks allow companies to gather more and more data from their own computers and networks. Storage costs are decreasing, allowing for more and more security monitoring data to be retained. Furthermore, the *infosec* community is becoming more aware of machine learning and other types of statistical analyses as mechanisms to gather new insights from existing data. However, more data doesn't automatically enable better analysis. In this book, we aimed to define a path by which artificial intelligence tools can enable security practitioners to make better sense of security data in order to make more reliable attribution decisions.

© The Author(s) 2018
E. Nunes et al., *Artificial Intelligence Tools for Cyber Attribution*, SpringerBriefs in Computer Science, https://doi.org/10.1007/978-3-319-73788-1_7

Printed in the United States
By Bookmasters